# Choosing Liberty in California Policy Reform

*Examining Affordable Housing, Euthanasia, Occupational Licensing, and School Choice in California.*

R. L. Cohen, PhD

3 Ravens Media

ISBN: 9781988557281

Published in the United States of America
Published by Three Ravens Media

# Table of Contents

**Chapter 3: The housing market in California: problems with its function and tentative suggestions for reform. . . . .89**

# List of Figures

# List of Tables

# CHAPTER 01

# The Role of Occupational Licensure in Creating Poverty and "Free" Ways to Get Out of It

# Introduction

A re the socio-economic conditions in which individuals live entirely the result of their own actions? It is impossible for a reasonable individual to answer yes to this question. Our socio-economic conditions are shaped by several factors that depend entirely on chance. The country of your birth, who your parents are, the kind of social environment you grew up in, the schools you attended, your natural talents, and whether you live in a society that values these talents are environmental factors that develop beyond your control. If environmental factors dominate a person's life, their control over what happens to them will be minimal. Responding to this reason, social programs aim to meet the basic needs of disadvantaged groups by providing financial aid without making any connection between individual actions and poverty.

However, public policies can address some environmental factors, increasing productivity and helping individuals live a more fulfilling life. The fact that South American migrants in the US quickly tripled their incomes reflects established economic and legal conditions in the US, not individual abilities. South American immigrants are more productive in the US than in their home countries, as the US offers better protection for their rights and freedoms, especially their economic freedom and private property. Hence, although many environmental factors cannot be changed, some can, and these will increase individual development significantly. These changes relate to public policies that promote the freedom to work, the personal development of individuals, and the protection of private property.

Compared to other states, California has generous social welfare programs. Federal and state anti-poverty programs in California spend more than $100 billion each year, representing nearly $15,000 per poor Californian (Tanner, 2021). However, California does not outperform other states in fighting poverty. Even before the pandemic, according to the US Census Bureau's Supplemental Poverty Measure, approximately 7 million Californians—17.2 percent of the State population—lived below the poverty threshold. This poverty rate is the highest in the country. Furthermore, the California Poverty Measure (CPM), co-produced by the Stanford Center on Poverty and Inequality and the Public Policy Institute of California, indicates that 35.2 percent of Californians live in poverty or are close to it (Tanner, 2021).

Do these statistics mean that the social safety net is ineffective in fighting poverty? The answer is both yes and no. Estimates suggest that in the absence of social programs, the poverty rate would be about 18 percent higher in California (Mattingly et al., 2019). Hence, the social safety net has a noticeable effect on reducing poverty. However, social programs still fail to eradicate relative poverty because their primary goal is to reduce the material deprivation of the poor, not to equip the poor with the talents and opportunities to create personal prosperity. The poor's access to adequate food, shelter, and healthcare takes precedence over other needs or emergencies (Tanner, 2021).

California's high poverty rate is not linked to its economy, as the state's GDP of approximately $3 trillion would make it the world's sixth-largest economy if it were a country. This figure indicates an annual per capita income of around $80,000. The average poverty threshold for a family of two adults and two children in California is $35,500 (United States Census Bureau, 2022).

Given these figures and the state's large, growing economy, why is poverty in California higher than the US average? This question could be answered at great length, but a brief list of the main factors that cause poverty provides immediate answers: high housing costs, unfair criminal laws, inadequate education and workforce development, poorly designed social programs, and exclusionary economic regulations. It would be easy to extend the list, but all these factors have a fundamental problem in common. Many laws, policies, and regulations intended to protect and help citizens contribute to the poverty cycle by limiting the productivity of the poor and their participation in the economy.

Therefore, it is impossible to eliminate relative poverty with anti-poverty policies alone. The challenge is to help Californians living in poverty become self-supporting and self-fulfilling individuals. Even though most environmental factors are beyond the control of individuals, the economic and political environmental conditions that facilitate wealth creation can be politically determined.

In a market economy, individual prosperity depends primarily on economic freedom and freedom of entrepreneurship. Not everyone has the chance to become Michael Jordon or Elon Musk. However, ensuring economic freedom and freedom of entrepreneurship for individuals and small business has nothing to do with unchangeable environmental factors. The secret lies in not hindering people's productive capacities and not preventing them from producing.

Poverty is not destiny, and pervasive poverty is not due to individuals' unwillingness to work. Widespread poverty arises when individuals are not provided with suitable economic opportunities or are excluded from them. If poor children become low-income adults in a growing economy, and upward economic mobility within specific communities is consistently low, the problem is primarily political, not economic.

Identifying California's poor reveals the political aspect of the poverty cycle. The rates of the state's poor by race are as follows: Latinos 22.9 percent, African Americans 18.2 percent, Asian/Pacific Islanders 15.9

percent, Multiracial 14.1 percent, and White 12.8 percent (Public Policy Institute of California, 2022; United States Census Bureau, 2022). The data shows that poverty is more prevalent among minorities and communities of color. Moreover, the poor's problem is not that they are unable to find jobs, but that they cannot earn enough to exceed the poverty threshold even though they work. African Americans and Latinos are at a clear disadvantage compared to other races in terms of upward economic mobility.

In this chapter, I argue that occupational licensure is one of the most important factors trapping minorities and communities of color in poverty. Costly and time-consuming licensure requirements place a heavy burden on low-income communities. It takes an average of 827 days to obtain an occupational license in California, and the average cost is $486 (Tanner, 2021). Much arbitrarily developed occupational licensure prevents low-income communities from entering more lucrative jobs and starting new businesses. For example, according to the Archbridge Institute, occupational licensing increases inequality according to the Gini coefficient by 12.77 percent in California while reducing upward economic mobility by 5.53 percent (Timmons et al., 2018).

Moreover, occupational licensing turns those who qualify for the license into an interest group and significantly reduces occupational competition. The many occupational licensing laws with severe conditions unrelated to protecting public health and safety prevent low-income people from entering high-paying jobs or starting a new business. While vested interests created through occupational licensure cause more severe conditions to be imposed on existing occupational licenses, groups that are not subject to license pursue new occupational licenses to exclude newcomers. This process leads to the creation of a rent-seeking society. The following sections explain the irrationality of professional licensing, exposing the arbitrary terms of most occupational licensure.

## What is Occupational Licensure?

Occupational licensure is a process by which a government defines the qualifications individuals must possess to practice a profession or trade. This situation means practitioners cannot legally practice their occupation or run their business without meeting these qualifications. Those who practiced their jobs without becoming licensed would pay a fine or face jail time (Little Hoover Commission, 2016).

Licensing can often be confused with certification and registration, but these are all distinct requirements. Certification is an act of accrediting professionals to demonstrate that they meet the qualifications set by the government or a legal organization. Individuals can practice their profession without obtaining a certificate, but it is forbidden to use the professional/occupational title without accreditation. Registration requires practitioners to provide the respective official organizations with their name and address and a description of their services in order to practice in a state. Thus, registration is a less restrictive occupational regulation than licensing and certification (Carpenter et al., 2017).

## Rationalization of Occupational Licensure

The proponents of occupational licensing claim that licensing procedures are intended to safeguard public health and safety by introducing mandatory educational requirements and industry oversight. It is also expected that licensing would support the career development of licensed practitioners through raising the quality of professions. The reason for unlicensed occupation posing a public health and safety threat is often referred to as an asymmetric information problem. Investopedia describes asymmetric information as follows:

> Asymmetric information, also known as "information failure," occurs when one party to an economic transaction possesses greater material knowledge than the other party. This typically manifests when the seller of a good or services possesses greater knowledge than the buyer; however, the reverse dynamic is also possible. (Asymmetric Information, 2021, p. 1)

A typical example of asymmetric information given in textbooks concerns second-hand car dealing. Since car dealers know more about the actual condition of the cars than the prospective buyers, the latter may be at a disadvantage. At first glance, this example seems to explain why consumers should be protected through licensing. In the modern economy, where the division of labor and specialization has grown tremendously, licensing any specialization in trade would result in a highly rigid and counterproductive economy. Such economic interventions foster a rent-seeking society, and every citizen is significantly harmed by such regulations.

Consequently, well-intentioned policies are not enough to stimulate a productive economy, as there are many unintended consequences that policymakers cannot predict. The methods discovered by markets to regulate complex economic transactions are often needed to overcome problems such as asymmetric information. The asymmetric information in car dealings is easily solved by free-market initiatives such as car inspection services and insured second-hand car sales. A strictly licensed second-hand car market would make entry into the market difficult and raise the prices of these services.

If all people sought such regulations to protect their businesses from market competition, everyone would suffer equally. Economists call this "the collective action" problem (Olson, 1971). If problems of trust between parties in economic transactions cannot be solved with market-oriented initiatives, political intervention in the economy will have to be requested. However, inviting politicians to regulate market transactions would create a society where everyone tries to live at the expense of everyone else. Since modern economies involve complex market transactions, even benevolent political intervention would bring malicious, unintended consequences. In fact, "asymmetric information is seen as a desired outcome of a healthy market economy in terms of skilled labor, where workers specialize in a trade, becoming more productive, and providing greater value to workers in other trades" (Asymmetric information, 2022).

## Who is Protected by Occupational Licensure?

The complex nature of market transactions might not justify the abolition of all occupational licensing for most people. When it comes to licensing, the first professions that come to mind for consumers are those that require higher education, such as physician, dentist or lawyer. A bachelor's degree is already required to practice these professions. However, in the USA, strict licensing requirements are demanded for a wide variety of occupations. Examples include florist, auctioneer, scrap metal recycler, gaming cage worker, tree trimmer, interior designer, door repair contractor, animal breeder, taxidermist, shampooer, weigher, bartender, animal trainer, home entertainment installer, dental assistant, hair braider and optician.

It is a little-known fact that hair braiding is considered a "risky" procedure that requires state licensing in some states. The hours involved in training to be a braider varies.

For example, in Louisiana in 2012, the required training was 500 hours. This means a hair braider could obtain a license in 62.5 days by training eight hours a day. In contrast, in Mississippi in 2012, a hair braider required no training. Thus, a hair braider from Mississippi would not be able to enter the market in Louisiana. This discrepancy is reflected in the fact that Louisiana had 32 registered hair braiders in contrast to 1,245 in Mississippi (Carpenter et al., 2017). A person who has learned African braiding from their family in its original cultural setting is not allowed by the government to earn a living as a hair braider in some states without formal training.

Shampooer is another licensed occupation in the USA. By definition, "shampooers shampoo and rinse customers' hair" (Institute for Justice, 2022e). The occupation sounds simple, yet 37 states believe it carries a potential risk to public health. Shampooers must complete 248 days of training and work experience and pass two exams to become licensed. Licensed shampooers must also pay a $130 fee. Imposing licensing requirements on shampooers may seem unnecessary, but it may be due to barbering and cosmetology boards wanting to keep shampooers under their occupational control.

The tree trimmer is another noteworthy example of occupational licensing. Although only seven states have made tree trimming a licensed profession, the requirements for the license are strict. For example, California requires that tree trimmers have 1,460 days of experience before they can accept jobs at or above $500. Tree trimming may be a profession that requires experience, but the requirement of four years of experience is arbitrary (Carpenter et al., 2017).

These are not just eccentric examples of an otherwise logical professional licensing situation. Many people might consider that licensing reflects rational and moral principles throughout the USA to protect the consumer and advance the various professions. However, this is not the case.

Occupational licensing in the USA has been increasing every year in recent decades. Occupations with the highest share of this increase are those that require less formal education and generate low and medium incomes. As of 2015, The Council of State Governments estimated that 1,100 professions were licensed, certified, or registered across the country. The number of licensed occupations in the USA increased from less than 5% in the 1950s to over 25% in 2015 (Goodwin & Symplexity Research & Consulting, 2017). In California, one in six employees is licensed. Research shows that workers are not leaving their factories or farms to move into previously licensed occupations, and many previously unlicensed occupations are now licensed. Most of the occupations affected are specific to the lower-income groups (Little Hoover Commission, 2016). This trend means that only those with time and money can access these licensed occupations.

I am against all occupational licensing. However, this section is not concerned with abolishing all occupational licenses in California or the USA. I am only opposed to licensing occupations with low and moderate returns that do not pose a threat to public health or safety. My main argument is that low and middle-income occupational licensing creates an unnecessary and irrational barrier to entry into these occupations, thus depriving disadvantaged individuals and communities of job opportunities.

After the explanations made so far, there are two crucial questions to be asked. First, which low and middle-income occupations are subject to licensing, making entry into the market more difficult? Second, which communities and groups suffer most from occupational licensing? I will briefly answer these questions with data based on scientific research.

## Arbitrarily Licensed Occupations

The second edition of License to Work, the research conducted by the Institute of Justice on low-income occupational licensure in 2017, lists licenses that are unnecessary and irrational in many respects (Carpenter et al., 2017). The report examined 102 low-income occupations in five different categories based on the requirements imposed on workers. The requirements categories are fees, education and experience, exams, minimum grade completed, and minimum age. The report also ranks the states that place the most burden on low-income occupations, considering the distribution of occupations surveyed across the 50 states and the District of Columbia. The report gives a separate licensing profile for each state, allowing comparisons to be made.

Interstate comparisons demonstrate the extent to which the licensing of occupations is regulated by arbitrary criteria. There are too many discrepancies between the licensed occupations to be rationally justified, both in terms of their mandatory requirements and the number of states in which they are regulated. The following sections list some of these inconsistencies.

## Interstate Comparisons of US Licenses

Only 27 of the professions examined in the License to Work report are licensed across the country. State governments have differing opinions on whether the other 75 occupations pose a threat to public health and safety. Even though the report states that 40 states license 23 occupations, there is an evident inconsistency in licensing between states. Furthermore, most of these occupations can be practiced without regulation in at least one state, and usually more than one. This detail suggests that most of these occupations do not inflict widespread harm. Another significant part of the data is the comparison between states with the most licensed occupations and those with the fewest. Colorado, Minnesota, Montana, South Dakota, Vermont, and Wyoming license up to 34 occupations listed in the report, while California, Louisiana, Nevada, and Washington license more than 74 (Carpenter et al., 2017).

Moreover, the same occupation licensed in different states can have different requirements. The report lists the 58 occupations with the most varying licensing requirements in terms of hours of education and experience. The estimated calendar days lost varies by 700 days or more among these occupations. For example, 30 states require less than 8 hours of training for a practicing head coach (in high schools) licensed by 49 states, while New York requires 1,125 days of training and experience. To practice as head coach in Arkansas, Georgia, Missouri, New Jersey, Ohio, Oklahoma, and Virginia requires being a licensed teacher. In other states, head coaches do not need to be licensed teachers (Carpenter et al., 2017).

The requirements for vegetation pesticide applicators depend on the state they live in. Even though this occupation is licensed in every state and DC, 31 states require no training or experience, while Delaware, Hawaii, Massachusetts, and Tennessee demand 730 days of experience (Carpenter et al., 2017). According to the U.S. Bureau of Labor Statistics (2021'), vegetation pesticide applicators "mix or apply pesticides, herbicides, fungicides, or insecticides through sprays, dusts, vapors, soil incorporation, or chemical application on trees, shrubs, lawns, or crops" (p. 197). A basic level of education is required to perform this occupation, but 730 days of experience requirement seems excessive. Moreover, people running such a business in New York must pay $3,000 and pass up to seven exams (Carpenter et al., 2017).

In the report, interior designers have the most burdensome licensing requirements. Despite three states and DC licensing the practice of interior design, the license requirements are challenging. To be a licensed interior designer requires 2,190 days of experience or education and a fee of up to $1,485 (Carpenter et al., 2017). The justification for this is far from clear.

The most erroneous practice regarding the licensing of low-income occupations is the requirement making it difficult to open a business based on these occupations. Even though governments allow people to practice an occupation as a paid worker without obtaining a license, in most cases they impose stringent licensing requirements on opening a business in that occupation. Among the 102 licensed professions, there are 34 contractor jobs (including sheet metal contractor, HVAC contractor HVAC contractor, drywall installation contractor, and door repair contractor) that show the restrictive nature of licensure in terms of entrepreneurship. Running a business is essential to enter an occupation and to encourage upward mobility. However, arbitrary requirements for running a business lessen individuals' entrepreneurial desires, reducing market competition and upward mobility.

## Examples from California

The License to Work report ranks states by the burden of licensure requirements. According to this ranking, the top three are Hawaii, Nevada, and California, with the latter having licensed 76 of 102 low-income occupations. In California, the average fee paid for licenses is $380, the average days of training and experience required for licenses is 827, and the average number of exams to pass to obtain licenses is two. These facts make California the most broadly and onerously licensed state in the USA (Carpenter et al., 2017).

The most striking problem with California's occupational licensing is the burdensome requirements placed on contractor jobs. The licensing of 34 contractor businesses poses a significant obstacle to the entrepreneurship of lower-income earners in the state. Furthermore, the burden of occupational licensing for mobile home installers, tree trimmers, midwives, animal trainers, pest control applicators, veterinary technicians, psychiatric technicians, cosmetologists, shampooers, makeup artists, skincare specialists, and manicurists is above the US average. Abolishing or changing these licensing requirements with less restrictive alternatives would significantly improve the conditions of low-income earners.

Another notable aspect of occupational licensing in California is the excessively regulated entry into occupations associated with cosmetology. These occupations are cosmetologist (373 days of experience and education), shampooer (350 days of experience and education), makeup artist (140 days of experience and education), skincare specialist (140 days of experience and education), and manicurist (93 days of experience and education). Considering that 37 days of education is sufficient to obtain an emergency health technician license, it is difficult to justify the 373 days of experience and education needed to obtain a cosmetologist license.

It is also informative to compare the requirements for manicurists and tattoo artists in California, as this reveals the arbitrariness of cosmetology licensure. Practitioners of these two professions are exposed to similar health risks, such as bacteria and fungi. However, manicurists must complete 400 hours of training and education and pay thousands of dollars in fees. Before being licensed, manicurists must pass written and practical exams. However, the practical exam is held in only two cities (Fairfield and Glendale), and manicurist candidates lose their fees and have to restart the training process if they fail to take the exam on the appointed date and time. In contrast, tattoo artists have to register with the public health department of their county, get the Hepatitis B vaccine, and submit blood test results for various diseases. The total cost of blood tests is 25 dollars (Little Hoover Commission, 2016). The most significant fact for manicurists is that they are under the jurisdiction of the cosmetology board. Otherwise, it is impossible to explain the difference between the licensure requirements of manicurists and tattoo artists.

Furthermore, when the demographics of manicurists are examined, it is apparent that the differences between the licensing requirements of these two professions are also a social problem. A study conducted in 2006 shows that

41 percent of manicurists across the USA are Vietnamese (Federman et al., 2006). California has had a relatively large number of Vietnamese manicurists since the 1990s, and it was Vietnamese practitioners who reinvented manicure practice in the USA. However, 30 percent of Vietnamese Americans are not fluent in English, and the requirements for registration in California are challenging for low-income Vietnamese. Unfortunately, in many occupational licensures, the state of minorities is no different from that of the Vietnamese manicurists.

As the explanations above reveal, people can be given more control over their lives and improve their quality of life if the barriers to individuals' aspiration to work are removed. Reducing or removing barriers to freedom of work would be most effective in California, because the California government restricts the freedom to work more than any other state. However, relative poverty could be quickly reduced in California with policies that expand the reach of freedom. The following section examines how arbitrary occupational licensing contributes to poverty and shows why more freedom is needed to reduce poverty.

## How Could Low-Income Communities Benefit from the Repeal of Many Occupational Licenses?

Despite the probability of licensing the professions increasing as the education level increases, occupational licensing affects lower-income communities disproportionately. The occupational licenses mentioned in this section are costly and time-consuming for those who want to begin new occupations. Individuals are forced to overcome many conflicting limitations in choosing the most suitable occupation in the most suitable place for them both professionally and geographically. These artificial barriers prevent market actors from shaping the most suitable career development according to the goods and services demanded in the market. As a result, labor productivity decreases, new jobs are blocked, and the prices of goods and services increase. Four out of five studies show that occupational licensure affects ethnic minorities disproportionately (McLaughlin et al., 2017).

## Conclusions of Scientific Research on Low-Income Occupational Licensure

According to the research conducted in 2006 by Kleiner, a leading occupational licensing expert, employment growth is lowest in places where occupations are licensed. Kleiner states that overall "the employment growth rate is approximately 20 percent higher in states that do not require licensing" (p. 149). Another study by Kleiner, published in 2015, demonstrates that occupational licensing can cause 2.85 million job losses annually. Moreover, due to occupational licensing, consumers may pay an additional $203 billion for their annual goods and services.

The Hamilton Project Report on occupational licenses explains why unlicensed workers bear a greater burden of unemployment: "…licensing creates 'crowding' in unlicensed occupations and labor scarcity in licensed occupations, driving a wedge between the unemployment rates in the two sectors" (Nunn, 2016, p. 7).

This finding implies that earnings are redistributed from unlicensed workers to licensed workers and that unlicensed workers disproportionately bear the burden of unemployment.

In relation to these unfair unemployment issues, another natural consequence of job losses and hindering entrepreneurship is rising prices. Since many factors affect employees' wages, it is not possible to quantify the relationship between wages and licensing. However, there is an average 12 percent difference in premium payments between states where occupations are licensed and where they are not (Klein, 2006).

One of the most detrimental consequences of occupational licensure for low-income communities is that it reduces the appetite for entrepreneurship. According to a study conducted in 2015, the rate of low-income entrepreneurship is 0.38 percent. This figure means that there are 380 entrepreneurs per 100,000 low-income earners. The average national entrepreneurship rate is 0.30 percent, the entrepreneurship rate is higher in low-income communities. Since entrepreneurship is a crucial element of upward mobility, the effect of occupational licensing on entrepreneurship is an issue that should be emphasized. The Goldwater Institute report on low-income entrepreneurship summarizes the issue as follows:

> … the higher the rate of licensure of low-income occupations, the lower the rate of low-income entrepreneurship. The states that license more than 50 percent of the low-income occupations had an average entrepreneurship rate that was 11 percent lower than the average for all states, and the states the licensed less than a third had an average entrepreneurship rate that was about 11 percent higher. (Slivinski, 2015, p. 1)

A nationwide study conducted in 2017 on the relationship between red taping and ten low-income occupations (athletic trainer, veterinary technician, cosmetologist, massage therapist, manicurist, aesthetician, emergency health technician, pest control applicator, security guard, locksmith) shows that higher red tape index scores hurt employment and severely decrease entrepreneurship (Flanders & Roth, 2017).

## Slowing Down the Mobilization of Lower-Income Workers

One of the most important elements of economic efficiency is the free movement of capital and labor. In the USA, governments' ability to significantly regulate the economy in their administrative districts makes it meaningful for workers and businesses to move between states to maximize their income and profit. However, in lower-income communities, occupational licenses take away this inherent advantage of the federal system and slow down the mobilization of lower-income workers. States vary widely in both the occupations they license and the requirements for licensing. Unlicensed employees may not be able to afford a license, and license holders may be reluctant to meet the new credentials. Therefore, it is difficult for workers and entrepreneurs to mobilize between states. As a result, licensed workers immigrate between states 30 percent less than certified workers (Nunn, 2016).

Lower-income communities are affected by the decreased geographic mobilization imposed by occupational licensure, and military spouses and veterans are particularly adversely affected. Military spouses whose partners often have to change states have significant problems due to their inability to transfer their licenses between states. According to research, 34 percent of military spouses have occupational licenses, and 19 percent have difficulty maintaining them. Married service members also state that they are badly affected by the situation of their spouses when making their career choices (Little Hoover Commission, 2016). Similarly, veterans have problems subordinating their military training to civilian licensing requirements (Little Hoover

Commission, 2016), which means that millions of people between the ages of 25 and 30 have difficulty finding a job. According to the 2020 CA Census, there are 1.8 million veterans in California, and their integration into civilian life should therefore be a priority for the Government of California (California Complete Count Census 2020, 2020).

## Protecting Public Health and Safety Without Occupational Licensing

As explained in the previous sections, most occupational licensure cannot be defended on the rational grounds of protecting public health and safety. Furthermore, the inconsistencies between occupational licenses and between state requirements show that licensing can easily be diverted from its purpose. Thus, when it comes to public health and safety related to occupations, licensing should be a last resort. There are many alternatives that do not involve the disadvantages of licensure and provide greater freedom to workers and entrepreneurs. In the literature, these options are divided into two categories: voluntary and regulatory/government intervention. The following section considers voluntary options, which are non-regulatory and non-market-oriented alternatives to licensure (Carpenter et al., 2017; Department of Treasury Office of Economic Policy et al., 2015; Little Hoover Commission, 2016; Tanner, 2021).

# Voluntary Options

## Market Competition

Even though it may seem counterintuitive, the first condition of protecting the consumer is to provide effective market competition. Increasing the quality of goods and services, decreasing their prices, and introducing technological innovations are features of competitive markets. Public health and safety requires more than the goodwill of market actors, the knowledge of bureaucrats, and the soundness of procedures. Without a significantly self-regulating market economy, it is impossible to raise the delivery of goods and services to the desired level. If the first requirement of self-regulated markets is to secure private property and economic freedom, the second requirement is free entry and exit to the market. Therefore, no market actor who is not compelled to impose constraints on their behavior within market competition can be guided to desired social behavior by bureaucratic procedures. Market actors constrained by market competition can be directed by bureaucratic regulations to various desirable social outcomes. If the regulations themselves impede market competition, they can become the plaything of some of the market actors.

Market competition is the primary mechanism that empowers consumers and protects them from fraud. As McCreadie (2009) asserted, a well-functioning economy must be based on legitimate self-interest, not goodwill.

Otherwise, there is no mechanism to control the market processes in which millions of people trade simultaneously, and it is not possible to unconditionally trust the goodwill of the people who are supposed to supervise this mechanism. For example, there are significant economic reasons why communist and centralized economic systems that eliminate market competition cannot provide public health and safety.

Furthermore, the technological progress that sets standards in different occupations and innovative practices originates from the free-market economy. The standards themselves, imposed by bureaucrats or legislators, would not exist without competitive markets. Thus, maintaining high standards in producing goods and services is closely linked to a productive economy, while a productive economy is closely tied to a free-market economy.

Legislators may wish to impose standards that cannot be easily afforded by the majority of consumers in various markets. However, there is no reason to believe that such standards are always in the best interests of the consumers. For example, dentists' demand for the closure of teeth whitening businesses for public health reasons is more about preventing market competition than consumer health. It is difficult to justify why products that can be bought from the market and applied at home should only be applied by dentists. The only consequence of this restriction is to double or triple the cost of teeth whitening (Erickson, 2013).

## Market-oriented Solutions to Asymmetric Information Problems

Apart from market competition, some other practices can protect customers from fraud. For example, in competitive markets, service providers want to maintain the credibility of their business by publishing comments from past customers. In addition, social media applications or online service review sites for each market provide consumers with information about the services and reliability of service providers. Reviews on online sales sites (Amazon, eBay, etc.) and applications for various services (Swarm, Trustpilot, etc.) provide better insight into service providers than most regulations could offer.

Some services may pose a risk to consumers regardless of market competition or company reliability. In risky business lines, companies voluntarily benefit from the services of bonding or insurance companies to eliminate trust issues and gain an advantage in the market. In this way, the customer's compensation is guaranteed when the contractor fails to complete the work or harms the customer. This application is widely used, especially in temporary personnel agencies companies (Carpenter et al., 2017).

## Government Interventions

Another important mechanism that does not regulate the market is that customers who suffer as a consequence of the services they receive can sue their service providers. The ability of citizens to seek their rights through legal means is a motivation that strengthens companies' self-control. For litigating service providers to be quick and practical, plaintiffs must be able to file lawsuits in the small claims court, and when the court justifies the plaintiff's claims, the defendant must bear the plaintiff's court and attorney costs. Addressing the deficiencies in the related laws and regulations by the legislature will contribute to customer safety. Reviewing deceptive trade practices and consumer protection laws in this context would be beneficial (Carpenter, 2017).

Inspection can be used in some settings instead of licensure. Regular random inspections can be performed to audit the work of technicians or craftspeople. For example, inspecting restaurants makes it possible not to license restaurant employees such as food preparers, waiters, and dishwashers. Expanding the scope of this approach may prevent new licensing requests (Department of Treasury Office of Economic Policy et al., 2015).

Governments may require mandatory bonding or insurance when the actions of service providers are likely to cause harm to third parties other than the customer. For example, Minnesota requires bonding for HVAC contractors. Thus, the state can regulate the contractors without hindering market competition. Bonding is a more effective method than licensing for entrepreneurs, customers, and the general public (Department of Treasury Office of Economic Policy et al., 2015).

Certification is the most restrictive occupational regulation among government interventions, but it is still preferable to licensure. Through certification, the government sends a message to prospective customers that certificated workers and companies meet specific standards. The bureaucracy required for the certification is time-consuming and costly, but it is still a more desirable option than licensing. Even though certification bans the usage of the title of the occupation, it lets entrepreneurs enter the respective market freely (Department of Treasury Office of Economic Policy et al., 2015)

# Personal Stories of Low-Income Workers

The theoretical and scientific explanations discussed above are clear, but it is still difficult to grasp the problems created by occupational licensure without understanding what real people are going through. The people whose stories are recounted in the following sections provide real examples of unnecessary restrictions on freedom to work.

## Ilona Holland

Ilona became a licensed massage therapist in Maryland in 2013. She and her family moved to Omaha, Nebraska, for family reasons. However, when Ilona wished to set up her practice in Nebraska, she was shocked to learn that she needed to take 400 hours of training to qualify as a massage therapist. She had assumed that the 600 hours of tutoring and ten years of experience required to gain her massage therapist license in Maryland would be considered in Nebraska, but this was not the case. Furthermore, Ilona's massage therapy training from a UK university and many of her health-related certifications over the years were not valid in Nebraska. Eventually, Ilona found a way to establish her business in the neighboring state of Iowa, which considers licenses obtained in other states when issuing massage therapist licenses. Thus, Ilona was spared from taking 400-hour courses and spending thousands of dollars unnecessarily (Independent Women's Forum, 2022a).

## Donna Harris

Donna is an occupational therapist and personal trainer with a bachelor's degree in nutrition. Donna's problems began when personal training clients asked her for nutritional advice on how to lose weight and stay fit. When Donna devised a general wellness program for clients, it was reported to the state board by a licensed dietitian. She received a cease-and-desist letter threatening six months in prison and/or a $1,000 fine. Even though Donna explained to the board that she does not claim to be a licensed dietitian and does not provide nutritional advice for any health condition, she could not change their decision. Donna is prohibited from giving nutritional advice to her clients (Professional Wellness Alliance, 2022).

## Natalie West

Natalie, a mother of two and a military spouse, earned bachelor's and master's degrees in social work. Operating as a social worker for 10 years, Natalie's career progress was hindered by the different occupational licensing criteria required by various states. She changes states every two to three years due to her husband's job as a career serviceman and struggles to have her education and work experience accepted by those states. When Natalie relocates, she often pays new fees and prepares for new exams, wasting time and money by not being able to work in the meantime (Independent Women's Forum, 2022b).

## Amanda Spillane and Courtney Haveman

Amanda and Courtney are two former convicts trying to start afresh. While in prison, they went to cosmetology school to gain new skills, and each paid $6,000 for the tuition. However, when they applied for a license to work in Pennsylvania after completing their time in prison, the cosmetology board decided they lacked "good moral character" and denied their license. Although Amanda and Courtney received job offers, they were not allowed to make a living in their preferred field of work (Institute for Justice, 2022d).

## Dario Gurrola

Dario, 38, from Northern California, works as a firefighter during the summer. His biggest goal is to find a long-term, non-seasonal job in this field. However, the emergency health technician license prevents him from getting a firefighter license. Because Dario was convicted of several crimes in his 20s, he has been denied a lifetime EMT license. Hence, the California government allows Dario to fight fires during the summer but excludes him from non-seasonal jobs in this field. Even though Dario received his firefighting training while in custody and California needs firefighters, the government has a ban. It is unconstitutional, arbitrary, and irrational to ban an ex-felon for life from work unrelated to their offence (Institute for Justice, 2022a).

## Free Speech Restrictions on an Online Real Estate Advertising Site

While licensing requirements prevent people from working, they can also restrict freedom of speech and the right to information. The online real estate advertising company ForSaleByOwner.com, founded in California, is not allowed to operate, because advertising real estate online can only be performed by a licensed real estate broker. Thus, the California government constrains citizens from freely expressing themselves and is prevented from accessing information that is vital to them. It could be argued that this prohibition is against the First Amendment (Institute for Justice, 2022b).

## The Brothers of Saint Joseph Abbey

In 2007, the brothers of Saint Joseph Abbey began manufacturing handmade coffins to support the institution's education and healthcare expenses. However, in Louisiana, licensed funeral directors have a monopoly on manufacturing and selling coffins, and it is a crime for others to do so. The monks had been making coffins for their brothers' funerals for generations, and the Abbey, which lost its forest lands after Hurricane Katarina, wanted to offer its coffin-making services to the public to replace their lost income. Coffins costing $1,500–$2,000 each were in great demand, until the funeral board forced Abbey to stop production. Fortunately, the monks' suit against the dispute was settled in 2011 in favor of Saint Joseph Abbey. US District Judge Stanwood R. Duval Jr. commented as follows: "There is no rational basis for the state of Louisiana to require persons who seek to enter into the retailing of caskets to undergo the training and expense necessary to comply with the rules of funeral director license" (Canfield, 2011, p. 1).There was no public interest in the licensed construction of caskets, but there was a considerable amount of private interest implicit in the funeral director license.

## Horse Teeth Floaters in Minnesota

Horse Teeth Floating is a traditional occupation for rural Minnesotans, many of whom are familiar with horse care. However, until it was amended in 2005, the Veterinary Practice Act stipulated that dental cleaning of horses, which is a safe and straightforward procedure, must be performed only by veterinarians. Because of this, many Minnesotans were excluded from this traditional line of work, and the price for the service was artificially increased. The Minnesota horse teeth floaters example demonstrates how college-educated professions such as veterinarians can unnecessarily expand their field of work (Institute of Justice, 2022c).

# Politics of Occupational Licensing

The evidence provided in this paper demonstrates the problematic aspects of occupational licensure, especially for low-income earners and consumers. It is paradoxical that market entry is so widely limited at the expense of public interest in the USA, where freedom of enterprise is championed.

## Abolishing the Romance of Politics

There are two fundamental reasons why political decisions can be taken at the expense of the people. The first is that politicians (including interest groups) and bureaucrats pursue their private interests when engaged in politics or providing public service. Public officials and politicians do not suddenly protect the common interest once they become involved with public services. This does not mean that politicians and bureaucrats always support their interests at the expanse of their fellow citizens (although this is a possibility) but that they have agendas that they try to achieve as rational individuals.

Government or public organizations cannot behave like individuals with their own ideas and interests. They are run by individuals with their own ideas and interests. Politicians and bureaucrats engage in public affairs as long as public organizations serve their goals. Therefore, public organizations cannot achieve predetermined social goals by acting like individuals. In particular, governments strike a balance between the often-conflicting interests of the many individuals and groups that influence political decisions. This situation is a common reason for the gap between governments' declared policy objectives and actual results. On the other hand, citizens falsely believe that when they ask governments to solve problems, politicians and bureaucrats take collective action without being affected by self-interest and personal agendas. Thus, understanding how political organizations work requires a rejection of this romantic definition of politics.

## Government Failure

Elected or appointed public officials are not always experts in their field, and a lack of knowledge can lead to flawed policies. In addition, political intervention in complex market relations may create economic and social problems beyond the comprehension and skills of experts. Economists call such results government failure, which is when governments fail to achieve their intended goals using legal and bureaucratic means. The results of government failures can be more costly than market failures. One vivid example of government failure is the fact that occupational licensure results in the opposite of its pre-declared goals.

The notion that public officials are also individuals pursuing self-interest has significant political consequences. The price increases and costs involved in occupational licensure are dispersed among many consumers, while the economic benefits are shared among very few practitioners. This disproportionate distribution of costs and benefits encourages service providers to organize at the expense of consumers. Politicians are also more sensitive to the interests of organized groups, because organized groups are more capable of supporting politicians' campaigns than unorganized broad masses. There is also no political backlash to unnecessary licensing, as licensing costs dispersed among many consumers go unnoticed and licensing is rationalized by professionals.

Those who legislate occupational licenses through lobbying are frequently board members for that licensure. Thus, those who defend the occupational licensure and those who decide how to apply it are the same people or those who share common interests. The vested interests created by the occupational licensure cause the licensed practitioners to want to expand their professional definitions continuously. For example, cosmetologists require shampooers to have a cosmetology license, veterinarians require horse teeth floaters to be veterinarians, and dentists demand that teeth whiteners be eliminated from the market (Carpenter et al., 2017).

## Sunrise and Sunset Reviews

The arguments presented in the previous sections support the notion that a policy cannot be supported simply by assessing the goodwill of the policy targets of politicians, interest groups, or bureaucrats. However, even if the intended goals of policies are accepted, the problem of unintended consequences arising from complex market relations cannot be ignored. To overcome the knowledge problem about the policies, policymakers have 'sunrise reviews' prepared for occupational licensure proposals and 'sunset reviews' to criticize existing professional licensure. Currently, 10 states, including California, have sunrise and sunset review laws, and 32 states have some form of sunset process (Department of Treasury Office of Economic Policy et al., 2015).

Studies show that sunrise reviews are more effective than sunset reviews in limiting occupational licensure. According to Thornton and Timmons (2015), only eight professional licenses have been repealed based on sunset review in the last 40 years. While sunset reviews generally recommend the continuation of a licensure, in cases where it is recommended to remove the licensure, the legislature has ignored the sunset recommendation (Department of Treasury Office of Economic Policy et al., 2015).

As is evident from the sunrise and sunset review process, policymakers must seek expert opinions on a specific law. However, it is likely that legislators do not always have the knowledge to evaluate expert opinions, and expert opinions might also be biased. Even if knowledgeable policymakers make laws based on objective research, it is not possible to monitor how future changes in the market alter the incentives of consumers and service providers. For example, technological innovations in service delivery can drastically change incentive structures in the markets. Therefore, existing laws can create economic inefficiency. For this reason, professional regulations affecting entry to markets should be designed as flexibly as possible, and it should be made less costly for market actors to adapt to new conditions. Otherwise, sunset review is often subject to manipulation by licensed experts.

In California, relevant committees demand sunrise criticism before a regulatory law is proposed. The key questions this critique tries to answer are:

1. Does the proposed regulation serve public health and safety?;
2. Is this regulation the most effective solution to the existing problem?;
3. What are the alternatives to the proposed regulation? (Little Hoover Commission, 2016).

In California, after implementing the relevant legislation, a sunset review of the regulation is conducted every four years. However, since 1986, only four of these reviews have requested changes to existing regulations, and regulations have often been reintroduced in different ways. Currently, most licensing in California is overseen by 40 boards, bureaus, commissions, and programs (Little Hoover Commission, 2016).

## Conclusion

The redistribution of income is the first policy that comes to mind when discussing the war on poverty. However, even though income redistribution may mitigate some of the symptoms of poverty, it is not a policy tool that will permanently increase the well-being of individuals. A generous social security policy based on redistributing income is not the feature that has attracted immigrants to America since colonial times. People have settled in America for the economic opportunities it offers them. Since the end of the 19th century, the USA has been the country with the largest, most creative, and most productive economy primarily because it does not exclude people from production processes but gives them the opportunity to work hard and save what they earn. In other words, American economic inclusiveness has been one of the main features that distinguishes the USA from the rest of the world.

Today, the USA is increasingly placing artificial restrictions on people's right to work in the name of occupational licensure, harming economic inclusiveness. Economic exclusion, which has increased rapidly in the last 50 years, has had the most significant effect on low-income communities and disadvantaged individuals and has contributed significantly to economic disparities in the USA. California, the state that puts the highest emphasis on social justice, has enacted the most widespread occupational licensure in the country for lower-income communities. These occupational licenses interfere most with the freedom of work of immigrants and communities of color and constitute the biggest obstacle to upward mobilization.

Unnecessary occupational licensure does not account for all the USA's poverty problems. However, the issue has widespread adverse effects that affect many people. Furthermore, many professional licensures are inherently anti-American, a violation of the American Constitution, and against individual freedom. Americans who sincerely care about income inequalities and poverty in the USA do not have the luxury of being indifferent to the upward mobility that economic freedom and freedom of enterprise can create in the lives of disadvantaged individuals. Artificial market entry barriers that hamper people's ability to lead a fulfilling life for themselves and their families must be removed. Ending the licensure of low-income occupations would be a positive first move in this direction.

# References

California Complete Count Census 2020. (n.d.). *Veterans*. California State. https://census.ca.gov/resource/ veterans/#:~:text=California%20is%20home%20to%20 over,state%20in%20the%20United%20States

Canfield, S. (2011, July 28). *Louisiana monks can keep making caskets*. Courthouse News Service. https://www.courthousenews.com/ louisiana-monks-can-keep-making-caskets/

Carpenter, D. M., II, Knepper, L., Sweetland, K., & McDonald, J. (2017, November). *License to work: A national study of burdens from occupational licensing* (2nd ed.). Institute for Justice. https:// ij.org/wp-content/uploads/2017/11/License_to_Work_2nd_ Edition.pdf?_ga=2.140390707.1816424755.1641804047- 704364518.1640113309

Department of Treasury Office of Economic Policy, Council of Economic Advisers & Department of Labor. (2015, July). *Occupational licensing: A framework for policymakers*. The White House. https://obamawhitehouse.archives.gov/sites/default/files/docs/ licensing_report_final_nonembargo.pdf

Erickson, A. C. (2013, April). *White out: How dental industry insiders thwart competition from teeth-whitening entrepreneurs*. Institute for Justice. https://ij.org/wp-content/uploads/2015/03/white- out1.pdf

Federman, M. N., Harrington, D. E., & Krynski, K. J. (2006). The impact of state licensing regulations on low-skilled immigrants: The case of Vietnamese manicurists. *The American Economic Review, 96*(2), 237-241. https://doi.org/10.1257/000282806777211630

Flanders, W., & Roth, C. (2017, March). *Fencing out opportunity: The effect of licensing regulations on employment.* Wisconsin Institute for Law & Liberty. https://will-law.org/wp-content/uploads/2021/01/FOO2-FINAL-v3.pdf

Goodwin, K, & Symplexity Research & Consulting. (2017). *The state of occupational licensing research, state policies and trends:Occupational licensing: Assessing state policy and practice.* National Conference of State Legislatures. https://www.ncsl.org/Portals/1/Documents/employ/Licensing/State_Occupational_Licensing.pdf

Independent Women's Forum. (2022a). *Ilona Holland: Regulations forced massage therapist to move across state lines to work.* https://www.iwf.org/chasing-work-ilona-holland/

Independent Women's Forum. (2022b). *Natalie West: State force social worker to start over.* https://www.iwf.org/chasing-work-natalie-west/

Institute for Justice. (2022a). *California firefighter fresh start.* https://ij.org/case/california-firefighter-fresh-start/

Institute for Justice. (2022b). *California internet real estate restrictions: A web of restrictions? Challenging California's free speech restrictions on internet real estate advertising sites.* https://ij.org/case/forsalebyownercom-v-zinneman/

Institute for Justice. (2022c). *Minnesota horse teeth floating: Challenging barriers to economic opportunity: Challeging Minnesota's occupation licensing of horse teeth floaters.* Retrieved from https://ij.org/case/johnson-v-minnesota-board-of-veterinary-medicine/

Institute for Justice. (2022d). *Pennsylvania fresh start: Law denies women right to work because of irrelevant criminal convictions.* https://new.ij.org/case/pennsylvania-collateral-consequences/

Institute for Justice. (2022e). *Shampooer.* https://ij.org/report/license-to-work-2/ltw-occupation-profiles/ltw2-shampooer/

Kleiner, M. M. (2006). *Licensing occupations: Ensuring quality or restricting competition?* W.E. Upjohn Institute for Employment Research. https://doi.org/10.17848/9781429454865

Kleiner, M. M. (2015). *Guild-ridden labor markets: The curious case of occupational licensing.* W.E. Upjohn Institute for Employment Research. https://doi.org/10.17848/9780880995023

Little Hoover Commission. (2016, October). *Jobs for Californians: Strategies to ease occupational licensing barriers* (Report No. 234). https://lhc.ca.gov/sites/lhc.ca.gov/files/Reports/234/Report234.pdf

Mattingly, M., Bohn, S., Danielson, C., Kimberlin, S., & Wimer, C. (2019, October). *Poverty declines in California, but more than 1 in 3 are poor or nearly poor.* Standford Center on Poverty and Inequality. https://inequality.stanford.edu/sites/default/files/california_poverty_measure_2017.pdf

McCreadie, K. (2009). *Adam Smits's the wealth of nations: A modern-day interpretation of an economic classic.* Infinite Ideas Limited.

McLaughlin, P. A., Mitchell, M. D., & Philpot, A. (2017, November). *The effects of occupational licensure on competition, consumers, and the workforce.* Meractus Center at George Mason University. https://www.mercatus.org/system/files/mclaughlin_mitchell_and_philpot_-_mop_-_the_effects_of_occupational_licensure_comments_for_the_ftc_-_v1.pdf

Nunn, R. (2016, June 21). *Occupational licensing and American workers.* The Brookings Institute. https://www.brookings.edu/research/occupational-licensing-and-the-american-worker/

Olson, M. (1971). *The logic of collective action: Public goods and the theory of groups* (Vol. 124). Harvard University Press.

Professional Wellness Alliance. (2022). *Case study: Dietary advice could mean jail time in Mississippi.* https://www.pwai.us/casestudy-donna

Public Policy Institute of California. (2022). *Who's in poverty in California?* Retrieved month day, year from https://www.ppic.org/interactive/whos-in-poverty-in-california/

Slivinski, S. (2015, February 23). *Bootstraps tangles in red tape: How state occupational licensing hinders low-income entrepreneurship* (Report No. 272). Goldwater Institute. https://goldwaterinstitute.org/article/bootstraps-tangled-in-red-tape/

Tanner, M. D. (2021). *Cato's project on poverty and inequality in California: Final report.* Cato Institute. https://www.cato.org/catos-project-poverty-inequality-california-final-report

U.S. Bureau of Labor Statistics. (2021, March 31). *Occupational employment and wages, May 2020: 37-3012 Pesticide handlers, sprayers, and applicators, vegetation.* Retrieved month day, year from https://www.bls.gov/oes/current/oes373012.htm

United States Census Bureau. (2022). *Quick facts: California City city, California; California; Los Angeles city, California* . Retrieved month day, year from https://www.census.gov/quickfacts/fact/table/californiacitycitycalifornia,CA,losangelescitycalifornia/IPE120220

## CHAPTER 02

# How School Choice Can Improve
the Academic Achievement of Low-Income
Students and Why It Matters

# How School Choice Can Improve the Academic Achievement of Low-Income Students and Why It Matters

One of the first structural reform targets in the fight against poverty is to increase the quality of education. There is a statistically significant relationship between education and income inequalities. Education and income inequalities are valid for underdeveloped and developed countries (De Gregorio & Lee, 2002). The importance of education stems from the fact that it is directly related to increasing individuals' talents and intellectual capital. Talented students are expected to become productive, creative, and high-income employees or entrepreneurs. A society with high social capital will be among the more productive and prosperous societies (van Ham et al., 2014). In today's competitive global economy, the quality of education is an issue that no government can ignore.

Another aspect of the importance of education is that regardless of the socioeconomic level of the community in which the student lives, access to quality education makes upward mobility between social classes possible.

Few things move society forward more than believing that students who invest in their talents and knowledge will have the chance to live the life they desire. Access to quality education can break the cycle of poverty and enable intergenerational upward mobility. Therefore, although education is valuable for all individuals, it is vital for low-income students.

However, it is a statistical fact that the academic achievement of public schools that enroll low-income students is worse than those that enroll middle and high-income students. Moreover, research shows that additional financial investment in schools in poor districts often fails to improve the quality of education (Petek, 2020, pp. 4–7). Hence, the failure of low-income students is explained by factors other than the education system, and it is emphasized that school failure is a complex phenomenon. The failure is not the fault of the education system but is linked to parents' and students' social capital inadequacies or policies that imprison parents in low socioeconomic environments.

Although there are complex reasons for school failure, changing the organizational form of public schools, introducing special practices for students, and giving families the chance to choose a school can significantly improve the students' success level, regardless of other factors. Many examples in the US and around the world demonstrate that low-income students' academic achievement can be improved by changing the organizational structure of traditional public schools (TPSs) and giving parents more choices.

The school choice system, including educational vouchers and charter schools, is the most well-known and controversial example of improving the quality of education by changing the organizational structure of public education. In the school choice system, the fund allocated per student for public education is given to parents as an education voucher to be used in private schools instead of allocating it directly to the TPSs. Parents can enroll their children in a school nominated by the government using an educational voucher. Parents' ability to choose causes the schools to compete to attract more students. Competition is an incentive not found in TPSs, and the chances of schools remaining open are closely tied to the academic improvement of their students. As I will examine in more detail below, the school choice system significantly increases the academic achievement of students, especially those from low-income backgrounds.

There are different school choice programs implemented in 42 states in the US (Veney & Jacobs, 2021, p. 1). Among these, charter school programs are the most widely implemented. California has offered charter school programs to students since 1992. The academic performance of TPSs in California is statistically below the US average, and the state is at the bottom of the academic achievement list. Academic failure is clearly detectable in California, especially among students with

African-American and Latino backgrounds. This data also reveals a significant disparity between different communities in terms of academic achievement. To ascertain the reason for this failure, it is necessary to examine the Californian public education system more closely.

## Are Public Schools Failing in California?

With 6.2 million students, California has the largest education system in the US, and the Los Angeles Unified School District is the second-largest school system in the country. California is at the top of the national list in terms of funds allocated to public education (Kaplan, 2017). The budget allocated to education in 2018–2019 was $97.2 billion, with approximately $12,000 spent per student. Thus, California's education spending per student is close to the US average of $12,612 (Hahnel, 2020).

Although the budget spent on public schools seems adequate compared to the US average, the academic performance of Californian schools ranks near the bottom. According to the National Assessment of Educational Progress (2019), California ranks 45th in student performance. According to the report of News & World, California schools are ranked 44th. These rankings show that the education system in California is well below average.

It is not difficult to find negative statistics on the Californian education system. For example, the state's rate of high school dropouts is 16.7% (World Population

Review, n.d.), which is the highest dropout rate in the US. According to American College Testing (ACT) benchmark scores, only 52% of Californian students are prepared for higher education in reading and math (Petek, 2020, p. 4). In the 2020–2021 school year, only 30.82% and 47.38% of eighth-grade students, respectively, met California's Smarter Balanced assessment benchmarks in math and English language arts. These rankings are below the national average (California Department of Education, 2021.

The problems with California's education system are even more severe when lower-income and minority communities are considered. There is a persistent disparity between students' performance in terms of both income and race. The disparity becomes more apparent when comparing African-American students with white and Asian students. According to the Legislative Analyst's Office (LAO) Report, in 2018, African-American students scored the lowest on standardized tests across all grade levels. Although Latino students outperformed African-Americans, they lagged behind white students. Asian students had test scores significantly higher than other groups in all respects (Petek, 2020, p. 5).

The achievement gap presents a similar disparity when income groups are considered. Students' family income and academic achievement are closely related. As family income increases, the success ranking within the income group also increases (Petek, 2020, p. 1).

Race and income factors are also valid in different educational success indicators. For example, 74% of African-American students and 94% of Asian students graduate from high school. While the rate of low-income white students graduating from high school is 78%, high-income African-American students' high school graduation rate is 78%. High-income Latino students have a high school graduation rate of 86%, while 87% of middle-income white students graduate. The achievement gap between race and income is consistent: 21% of African-American students, 35% of Latino students, 54% of white students, and 74% of Asian students meet college readiness benchmarks after graduation in California (Petek, 2020, pp. 5–7). Similar figures are valid for absenteeism rates.

Another claim supported by data is that low-income students have an increased chance of success when they attend the same school as high-income students. According to a study conducted in 2010, the income level of the students' classmates is as influential as the income level of their family in the students' success. For this reason, it is a statistical expectation that the success rates of schools enrolling low-income students are low (van Ewijk & Sleegers, 2010). Because California's schools are increasingly segregated in line with income groups, many low-income students have a disadvantaged start to their educational life. The de facto segregation in Californian schools is more salient for Latino students. In 1970, 54%

of students in schools enrolling Latino students were white, while currently, 84% of schools enrolling Latinos are nonwhite (de Brey et al., 2019, pp. 57–58).

The increasing segregation of schools in California in line with different social classes and races makes academic success an issue that cannot be solved by simply increasing funding. Indeed, California has reduced income disparities between schools in different districts with state funds, but this has made little impression on the success rates. In addition, the Local Control Funding Formula (LCFF), which came into force in 2013, allocates additional funds per student to schools in a high-need category (California Department of Education, 2021).

Therefore, the academic achievement gap among schools is not simply due to a lack of funds. For example, according to the CalMatters report in 2020, the impact of additional money spent on English language learners' academic achievement is mixed (Cano & Hong, 2022). While the level of success in some schools had increased relatively in 2020, most schools had not achieved significant improvement. The California State Auditor's Report of 2019 also showed that supplemental and concentration funding is not always used to benefit disadvantaged students (California State Auditor, 2019, pp. 1–4). Therefore, it is not possible to achieve academic success with additional funding without structural changes in the education system.

Although research on the relationship between funding and school performance offers different results, how money is spent is more important to academic success than simply spending money. Special academic programs and educational methods may need to be developed for respective students, particularly in cases where academic performance is closely related to social capital. It is much more difficult for English language learners, students with disabilities, low-income students, or underserved students of minority communities to improve their academic scores by following the standard academic programs implemented statewide. In California, where poorly performing schools and low-income districts often overlap, simply raising funds for TPSs will not improve academic performance. Instead, additional financial resources need to be spent in the context of educational reform.

It is difficult to give precise directions for educational reform. However, meeting the significantly varied educational needs of students from different socioeconomic statuses and social backgrounds with a centralized, traditional school system is unrealistic. In this respect, there are many reasons for reforming California's underperforming public school system by highlighting the specific needs of low-income students and students from underserved communities. Charter schools and educational vouchers are an option that should be considered within the scope of educational reform, as they both offer choice to parents and enable schools to organize according to the unique characteristics of the students.

To examine the possibilities that school choice offers for California's public school system, I will first make some remarks on the theory, history, and performance of school choice. I will then discuss the development, performance, and opportunities of charter schools in California.

## What Is School Choice?

Milton Friedman's 1955 article "The Role of the State in the Education Sector" provoked intense debate on the government's role in the education sector. Friedman argued that the financing and organization of public education at primary and secondary levels should be separate, and the organization part should be performed by private education institutions operating in the free market. While Friedman justified the publicly financed primary and secondary education for specific political and social reasons, he also stated that there is no compelling reason for organizing K-12 education through public schools. Furthermore, Friedman argued that leaving the provision of public education to competing private schools would be in the public interest and would greatly benefit the quality of education (Friedman, 1992, pp. 22–36).

Friedman offers two reasons, one normative/moral and the other utilitarian, to justify the educational voucher. He believed that parents should have more choice and control over their children's education. Students' attendance at schools that are limited with their demographics and the exclusion of parents from the school administration are violations of parental rights. Thus, the question of whether parents or bureaucratic organizations have more say over students' education is central to the moral aspect of the school choice system. The moral challenge posed by this system to the traditional outlook of public education has spawned an ongoing philosophical debate between those who advocate the traditional school system and those who advocate greater choice in education.

The demand for more choice in education has a further impact that calls into question the future of the traditional school system. The absence of competition in public education prevents the emergence of the incentives necessary to improve the quality of education and hinders innovative educational methods. Educational central planning and the lack of freedom of choice are the main reasons why public education organization does not differ much from the 19th-century model. It is difficult to find another sector that has been able to protect itself from such changes for 200 years. The fact that education entrepreneurs cannot innovate the education system according to the needs of students and the knowledge and skills demanded in respective societies over time proves how potent the myth of public education is. Otherwise, it is difficult to explain how public education has avoided being challenged by alternatives despite the dismal failure of public schools.

Friedman's school choice or educational voucher proposal has become an education reform phenomenon that finds supporters worldwide. In addition to school choice programs in various US states, it has been widely implemented and achieved significant success in Chile, Colombia, India, Sweden, Norway, and various Eastern European countries. Education voucher programs are open to all students in some countries (including Sweden, Chile, and the Netherlands) and some parts of the US (including Washington D.C., Florida, Milwaukee, and Cleveland). However, the program is generally available to low-income, poor-performing minority students or special education students to mitigate the achievement gap between social classes.

Along with the charter school programs, there are different school choice systems in the US. An education voucher is a scholarship paid to parents by the government, private benefactors or charity organizations to cover some or all of the fees at private schools (Walberg, 2007, p. 48). Although there are different scholarship programs in different countries, the education voucher is universally based on the principle that private schools compete to gain the education voucher per student, as determined by the government. Private education institutions that want to participate in this system can be included if they fulfill the terms set by the public organization established by the government to regulate the system.

The public organization adopts a standard curriculum but does not interfere with the school's education method, staff selection, or management. Private schools can hire employees and adapt their wage policy as they see fit. While private education institutions can operate for profit, they can also run private education institutions for ideological purposes. Private institutions that provide education for such purposes generally provide religious education, but some organizations work for the benefit of disabled children who need special education. However, it is a statistical fact that institutions included in the education voucher system are generally for-profit organizations. The main reason for this is that the profit incentive makes the process of organizing easier to organize. The public organization responsible for the education voucher often restricts the profit margin by prohibiting an extra charge on the voucher.

In addition, private education institutions cannot discriminate against students on any basis. A parent who has received an education voucher can enroll their children in any private school within the system. Apart from the profit motive, educational institutions compete to attract more students to their schools through education quality and the opportunities provided to students.

After examining a Swedish example, I will discuss school choice programs in the US and their impact on student performance. Sweden's education voucher system attracts great attention from parents and is rapidly spreading throughout the country. Moreover, the fact that

Sweden, a champion of welfare statism, continued to support the educational voucher system during the tenure of its social democratic governments makes the country an insightful example.

## Example of a Non-US School Choice Program: Swedish Independent Schools

Since 1990, primary and secondary education in Sweden, including all financial responsibility, has been organized by local governments, and the education system has been largely decentralized. After this education reform by the social-democratic government, the center-right political party, which won the 1991 elections, began the era of "choice" in education, thereby deepening this reform. In 1992, the education voucher system was introduced. It covered all students, regardless of income. Moreover, the Swedish government has allowed any entrepreneur who meets the terms defined by the National Education Institution to run a private education institution, leading to radical reform in the Swedish education system.

Private schools in Sweden can collect education vouchers from municipalities, and they are calculated based on the average cost per student. Private schools cannot demand fees from parents other than the education voucher, and they cannot discriminate on ethnic, religious, or socioeconomic grounds (Sahlgren, 2010, p. 6). After the education reform in 1992, 16% of students were subject to compulsory education, and 29% of students attending non-compulsory upper secondary schools attended independent private schools. Independent schools are private schools that accept education vouchers, and they are divided into for-profit and nonprofit schools. For-profit schools represent around 50% of independent schools (Sahlgren, 2010, p. 15).

It was predicted that the educational voucher system in Sweden would improve the quality of education in two ways. First, independent schools are expected to outperform local government schools due to competition in the free market. This situation is expected to become even more evident with the transfer of Swedish students from local government schools to independent schools. Second, local government schools that compete with independent schools have more incentive to improve their performance (Sahlgren, 2010, p. 7). However, this assumption is not always valid, especially since the funding of local government schools and the personal rights of teachers are guaranteed regardless of the number of students. As a result, local government schools can protect themselves from competition. The best way to measure the performance of independent schools is to compare the Grade Point Average (GPA) scores of students during secondary education. The GPAs are published every year, and they are a reliable method for comparing the success of schools in different categories. Striking results are obtained when schools are classified according to their ownership structures, taking into account the GPA.

The average GPA scores of schools according to their ownership structures for 2013 were as follows:

## Table 1

*GPA of schools according to ownership structures in 2013*

|  | Local government schools | For-profit independent schools | Nonprofit independent schools | Independent schools (established before 1992) |
|---|---|---|---|---|
| Average GPA score | 206 | 223 | 231 | 239 |

According to GPA scores, the most successful educational institutions are independent schools established before 1992. Since these schools represent 1% of the system, they have less weight than the others. However, the success of private schools, which are not subject to the limitations of the education voucher system, is remarkable. While nonprofit independent schools outperform for-profit ones, these nonprofit schools far outperform local government schools in terms of GPA scores. According to Sahlgren (2010), while families' socioeconomic backgrounds play a role in children's success, second-generation immigrant children are noticeably more successful than first-generation ones. A 10% increase in the number of students in schools induces a 2% increase in the GPA scores of students in local government schools.

In 2010, rhe average increase in the GPA scores of students enrolled in independent schools has been 21%, while the average increase in math scores has been 33% (Sahlgren, 2010, p. 8). Competition has increased the scores of local government schools. However, according to Sahlgren, the effect of independent schools is not seen in regions that are not directly exposed to competition. Regarding whether the education voucher system discriminates between students, it is evident that discrimination only occurs in the neighborhood where the families live (Sandström, 2005, p. 32). This type of discrimination seems to have decreased since the no-choice era. It is noteworthy that low-income students have benefited most from independent schools. Sweden has high levels of social cohesion and can easily compensate for socioeconomic variables, reducing the difference in academic achievements between low and high-income groups.

Edmark and Persson's (2021) study revealed that students included in the school choice system have a significant advantage over those in municipal schools. The researchers summarized their study results as follows: "To sum up, the independent school effects that we document in this study consistently indicate that attending an independent school on average benefits the individual in terms of grades, graduation rates, and post-secondary studies" (Edmark & Persson, 2021, p. 13).

# School Choice in the United States

The school choice system in the US involves two approaches: charter schools and educational voucher programs. I will discuss how each of these models works and to what extent they are effective.

## Charter Schools

Charter schools are public schools of choice and are funded by the governments. However, unlike TPSs, charter schools can receive public funds from the government for each student enrolled. Students can choose charter schools outside the borders of their districts. Charter schools cannot demand tuition fees or subject students to entrance exams. When the number of students applying to charter schools exceeds the quota, the students are usually registered to the school by drawing. Over one million students are currently waiting to enroll in charter schools (National Alliance for Public Charter Schools, 2014, p. 1).

The significant advantage of charter schools is that they are exempt from most of the legal restrictions that public schools are subject to, such as syllabus preparation and teaching methods. Thus, charter schools can adapt to new "environmental changes" without obtaining the permission of a higher education authority. In these schools, teachers are encouraged to discover new ways of increasing students' success. The cooperation established between parents, teachers, and students is the core of the performance increase in charter schools. In addition to such freedoms, charter schools are obliged to realize the founding purpose of the school within a certain period. Otherwise, the local authority may terminate the school's charter, and the school might be closed.

The main target of charter schools, especially in poorer districts, is to narrow the academic achievement gap. Schools that fail to do so may lose their students and financial resources and be closed by local authorities (Finn et al., 2000, p. 136). According to research by the National Alliance, the reasons for closing schools are low student enrollment, poor educational attainment, and financial difficulties. However, enrollments in charter schools are increasing, while student enrollments in TPSs are declining. First introduced in Minnesota in 1992, this system has been in use for over 30 years.

In the 2019–2020 school year, 44 states and Washington D.C. adopted the charter school system. Approximately 3.4 million students are enrolled in more than 7,700 charter schools. Charter schools currently account for 7.2% of public schools. The number of students enrolled in charter schools in 2020–2021 increased by 7%, largely due to the Covid-19 pandemic. According to Veney and Jacob (2010), charter school enrollment increased in 39 of 42 states during the 2020–2021 school year. However, student enrollment in district schools (TPSs) has dropped drastically. In the same period, student enrollment in California charter schools increased by 2.3%, while student enrollment in TPSs decreased by 3.2% (Veney & Jacobs, 2021, p. 3).

In the 2020–2021 school year, Californian charter schools were significantly preferred over TPSs according to racial and ethnic group distribution. For example, between 2019 and 2021, the number of Asians in charter schools increased by 1,252, while 4,454 Asian students dropped out from TPSs. Likewise, while the number of Hispanic students in charter schools has increased by 9,389, the number of Hispanic students leaving TPSs has reached 70,287 (Veney & Jacobs, 2021, p. 12). Racial and ethnic statistics are significant, because one in five students enrolled in charter schools is in California, and the state has the largest number of charter schools nationwide (White & Hieronimus, 2022).

However, charter schools are concentrated in urbanized areas, and the concentration in urban areas has been increasing over the years. In the 2010–2011 school year, 16% of the charter schools were in rural areas. In 2020–2021, 58.3% were enrolled in charter schools in cities, while only 9.4% were enrolled in charter schools in rural areas (White & Hieronimus, 2022). These rates justify the criticism that charter schools are an urban phenomenon to a certain extent. However, it is to be expected that students from low-income minority groups, who favor charter schools, are concentrated in cities. For example, the demographics of California, New York, and Florida, which have a significant number of charter schools, fit this pattern. In these three states, students enrolled in contract schools in 2019–2020 constituted 33.7% of total student numbers (White & Hieronimus, 2022).

## Performance of Charter Schools

There is abundant literature on the performance of charter schools. I will discuss how charter schools have been able to achieve the aims of their founding philosophy by making a brief review of scientific studies conducted at a national and state-specific level over the years. I will examine studies of charter schools published after 2010 and then focus on more recent studies.

Between 2010 and 2013, 16 independent studies were conducted on the performance of charter schools. Of these, four were national studies, and 12 were regional studies. In 15 of the studies, students attending charter schools performed better than students attending traditional schools (Separating Facts & Fictions, 2014). One study produced no conclusive results. Stanford University's Center for Research on Educational Outcomes (CREDO) has been conducting studies on US charter schools for more than two decades, revealing valuable information on school choice. This section focuses on CREDO's (2013) study of 16 states (Arkansas, Arizona, California, Colorado, the District of Columbia, Florida, Georgia, Illinois, Louisiana, Massachusetts, Minnesota, Missouri, New Mexico, North Carolina, Ohio, and Texas). This study is noteworthy as it compares the performance of charter schools and TPSs across different racial and income criteria.

The main question in the research was, 'How did the academic growth of charter school students compare to similar students who attended traditional public schools?' The students' academic achievement was determined according to the national standardized test scores in reading and math. The differences in the annual academic achievements of the students were primarily expressed using standard deviation, which is a statistical method. The standard deviation was expressed as days of learning to make it easier for the general reader to understand. For example, a standard deviation figure of 0.1 growth was converted to seven days of learning.

In this context, charter schools' effect on students' reading scores is positive and salient, with charter students gaining seven additional days of learning in reading compared to TPS students. Charter students lose seven days of learning in math compared to TPS students. Although charter school students have made significant progress regarding days of learning in math, compared to 2009 scores, they still perform worse than TPS students (CREDO, 2013, p. 29).

When these very general academic achievement CREDO results are detailed in line with the students' race and income group, the charter schools' performance differs significantly from TPSs. As charter schools in most states are expected to help underserved student populations, the results are promising.

According to the research charter, African-American students have seven additional days of learning in reading compared to their TPS counterparts. African-American students' math scores do not differ according to the school they attended (CREDO, 2013, pp. 32–33). However, it is observed that the academic success of African-American students improved as the years of study in charter schools increased.

Latinos are one of the largest communities in the US. When examined regardless of income group, charter Hispanics have seven fewer days of learning in both reading and math than Hispanic counterparts attending TPSs (CREDO, 2013, pp. 34–35). However, when Hispanics are separated according to income group and immigration status, the significant success of charter schools is revealed:

> Hispanic students in poverty have better learning gains at charter schools than at TPS, but non-poverty Hispanic students at charters have lower learning gains than their TPS peers (see Figure 34). In reading, Hispanic charter students in poverty have 14 more days of learning than similar TPS students, while Hispanic charter students who are not in poverty experience seven fewer days of learning per year than similar

TPS students. The differences are even larger in math. Hispanic charter students in poverty have 22 more days of learning in math than similar TPS students, while Hispanic charter students not in poverty experience 29 fewer days of math learning gains than similar TPS students. (CREDO, 2013, p. 68)

Moreover, the academic success of Hispanic and African-American students in poverty who attend charter schools in urban areas is more salient (CREDO, 2013, pp. 68–69). However, the striking academic success of Hispanics in poverty is not limited to the data above. Hispanic English language learners attending charter schools (i.e., recently immigrated Hispanic students) gained 50 additional days of learning in reading compared to their counterparts in TPSs (CREDO, 2013, p. 71).

Therefore, when the success of charter schools is evaluated in the context of students' socioeconomic status, the academic achievement gap experienced by these students is more apparent. Students from diverse communities, such as students in poverty, English language learners, and special education students, have different academic needs from the achieving students. Charter schools have the organizational freedom necessary to develop academic programs suitable for these students. Charter schools are more advantageous for these students than traditional schools in this regard.

Regardless of racial background, Charter students have 14 additional days of learning in reading compared to their TPS counterparts. Charter students in poverty have 22 additional days of learning in math (CREDO, year, pp. 36–37). English language-learner charter students, on the other hand, experience 43 additional days of learning in reading and 36 additional days of learning in math (CREDO, 2013, p. 38). Special education charter students have 14 additional days of learning compared to their TPS counterparts.

According to CREDO, charter schools are more advantageous for students in poverty than their TPS counterparts. However, the difference is not enough to close the achievement gap between disadvantaged and affluent students. It has also been found that success rates increase when charter students in poverty have been in charter schools for longer periods:

> Learning gains improve significantly for charter students by their second year of enrollment – seeing about 22 more days of learning in reading and 14 more days in math. Once a student is enrolled for four or more years, their learning gains outpace TPS by 50 days in reading and 43 days in math per year. (CREDO, 2013, p. 79)

CREDO's more recent charter school studies have delivered broadly similar results. For example, the 2020

CREDO charter school research conducted throughout Washington demonstrates that charter students perform significantly better than their TPS counterparts in the same district (CREDO, 2020). Research conducted in 2019 shows a severe academic performance decline, primarily due to the Covid-19 pandemic and online education. In South Carolina and New Mexico, charter school programs underperformed, particularly in math. However, the results of the CREDO study conducted between the 2011–2012 and 2014–2015 school years are significant in terms of charter school performance. According to research published in 2017, charter students gained 23 additional days of learning on average. This achievement is even more significant when charter Hispanic and African-American students are compared to their TPS counterparts. Moreover, students attending charter schools affiliated with the Charter Management Organization (CMO) gained 57 additional days of learning in reading and 103 additional days of learning in math (CREDO, 2017).

In the context of students' racial and income status, New York's charter schools are phenomenally successful. Thomas Sowell's (2020) book *Charter Schools and its Enemies* compares the performance of TPSs with that of five charter school networks housed together in New York. Sowell chose to conduct his study on TPSs and charter schools housed together to better compare same-status students' academic achievements by taking social, economic, and racial variables into account. The results highlight the tremendous success of charter schools, specifically for lower-income minority students.

A study conducted in 2013 by The Knowledge Is Power Program Charter School (KIPP) in Oklahoma is encouraging in regard to the success of low-income students. In Oklahoma, 75% of charter students were in racial minority groups, and 90% were low-income. All students have passed the eighth-grade state reading exam and graduated from high school. These facts are important indicators, as failure to graduate from high school is a severe problem in some parts of the US. Fourth-year students have averaged above the Oklahoma average in reading, math, and science exams. Significantly, 65% of students enrolled in a college after high school have no family members with a college degree (Tuttle et al., 2013).

## Education Vouchers

An education voucher is a program that donates some or all of private school tuition fees to parents. The vouchers are provided by government or private institutions. Scholarships provided by private companies, foundations, or philanthropists are called private vouchers, while scholarships provided by public institutions are called public vouchers.

In 2021, there were 27 scholarship programs in 16 states and Washington D.C. Around 220,000 students attend these programs (Education Commission of States,

2021). The education voucher scheme was originally inspired by Milton Friedman's ideas. It is smaller than the charter school system in terms of scale and number of students, indicating the opposition to the education voucher system in the US. However, despite political opposition, the application of education vouchers continues to grow.

Many studies have examined the education voucher system. By 2011, 10 national studies had stated that education vouchers improve students' academic performance. Six of these studies stated that the vouchers have positive effects not only on the participant students but on all students in the education system. Three studies suggested that the system is only effective for participant students. Only one study suggested that educational vouchers have no effect (Forster, 2016, p. 8).

A few examples from these studies serve to illustrate the positive effects of education vouchers. Howell and Peterson of the University of Wisconsin researched private education voucher programs in Dayton, New York, and Washington, D.C. According to their study, students in the Washington D.C. program received an overall 7.5 point increase in math and reading scores in two years. No observable change was found in Dayton over the same two-year period, but an increase of 6.5 points in two years was found for African-American students' math and reading scores. There were no observable changes for non-African-Americans.

Barnard, Hill, and Rubin presented an analysis for New York using Howell and Peterson's data. They found that a failing student who left TPS to enroll in an educational voucher program gained five points in a year. In 2010, Patrick Wolf of the University of Arkansas found that public education vouchers increased graduation rates by 12% in Washington D.C. Of the students who received the vouchers, 82% graduated, compared to 70% in the control group (Forster, 2016, p. 13).

Further insightful data comes from research conducted in the Edgewood school district of San Antonio, Texas, in 2013. All educational services in the low-income Edgewood school district operated in a Friedmanian fashion with a private education voucher program. Controlling for demographics and local sources, a comparison revealed that the Edgewood school district outperformed 85% of other education districts in Texas (Merrifield & Gray, 2013, pp. 127–142). Given that over 90% of this district comprises Hispanics in poverty, it is clear how significant this success is.

A meta-analysis analyzing the results of 21 studies covering eight US and three Indian education voucher programs reached results that conform to the example given in the previous paragraph. Moreover, no negative effects of education voucher programs on TPS students have been found (Kaitlin et al., 2021, pp. 531–532).

These results have encouraged parents to support school choice programs in the US. However, educational voucher programs have not spread as quickly as charter schools. While educational voucher programs promise further success, both in theory and in practice, leaving the organization of education entirely to free markets is still considered a radical idea by most Americans. For most politicians, more autonomous and competitive public schools seem more feasible than education voucher programs.

## California's Charter School Experience

Studies in California show that low-income minority students attending charter schools perform better than their TPS counterparts. The research conducted by CREDO in 2014 provides important data. Charter African-American students were shown to have gained 22 additional days of learning in reading and seven additional days of learning in math compared to their TPS counterparts (CREDO, 2014, p. 23). Similarly, low-income Hispanic charter students gained 22 additional days of learning in reading and 29 additional days of learning in math compared to their TPS counterparts (CREDO, 2014, p. 29).

On average, charter students in poverty gained 14 additional days of learning in reading and 29 additional days of learning in math compared to their TPS counterparts (CREDO, 2014, p. 29). Charter students receiving special education gained 36 additional days of learning in reading and seven additional days of learning in math (CREDO, 2014, p. 32). English language learner charter students gained 36 additional days of learning in reading and an additional 50 days of learning in math (CREDO, 2014, p. 33).

A 2019 joint study by the University of Southern California and Innovate Public Schools found that 27% and 57% of the top-performing schools in Los Angeles and the San Francisco Bay Area, respectively, were charter schools. While charter schools constitute 10% of schools statewide, 18% of top-performing schools statewide are charter schools (Innovate Public Schools, 2019). African-American and Hispanic charter students apply to University of California schools at a higher rate than their TPS counterparts and are accepted at twice the rate, according to a 2018 report by The California Charter Schools Association (California Charter School Policy Task Force, 2019).

In California, the accomplishments of low-income and minority students in charter schools are vital in mitigating the disparity created by the achievement gap. Although the performance of charter schools varies from district to district and school to school, the dissemination of successful school models and the discovery of more innovative practices depend on the expansion of charter schools.

Although California has above-average latitude in terms of charter school regulations, it is concerning that the California State Legislature discussed a moratorium on new charter schools in 2019. Some regulations, such as AB1505 and AB1507, make it difficult for new charter schools to open (California Legislative Information, 2019). Considering the achievement gap between underserved and advantageous communities in California, political decision-makers should endeavor to broaden school choice opportunities for low-income failing students, rather than limiting the options with short-term political concerns.

The great success of charter schools in improving the performance of low-income and minority students cannot be overstated. However, charter schools in California still have funding problems compared to TPSs. Charter schools in poorer districts have significant disadvantages compared to those in affluent districts. If additional funds are to be used to mitigate educational disparities among different communities, using these financial resources for charter schools in poorer districts will be more effective than other alternatives. In particular, California needs to compensate for the reduction in property taxes with the enactment of Proposition 13, since property taxes are the primary source of education funding.

In addition, although LCFF provides additional financial resources to schools in an attempt to close the achievement gap, approximately 20% fewer funds are allocated to charter schools enrolling high-need students compared to TPSs (Ugo & Hill, 2017). Some charter schools are reluctant to accept disadvantaged students because of this lack of funding (Ugo & Hill, 2017, p. 4). In California, where de facto segregation is common, public education needs to take a more privileged approach to financially disadvantaged student districts. Otherwise, disparity among students is likely to increase.

Although charter schools' performance is promising for low-income students, the school choice system can be further expanded with education voucher programs. Charter schools are more innovative than TPSs, but many regulations limit the organizational capabilities of charters. In contrast, private schools are exempt from many of the limitations that charter schools face and perform better than public schools (Coulson, 2009, pp. 31–54). In this context, allowing education voucher programs to run in California will involve minimal cost to public revenues, but its advantages to low-income students will be significant. Thus, private scholarships and the establishment of tuition tax credit programs that enable low-income students to attend private schools are essential for California. While the state has little to lose by adopting education voucher programs, there could be substantial gains for many students.

## Conclusion

The K-12 education system in the US is in crisis, and this crisis is a significant risk factor for the US economy and democracy. The ability of the American economy to maintain its position in the world depends on the country continuing to produce high-tech products with high added value. In this respect, the need for quality higher education and educated workers in the US is perpetual.

However, it does not seem possible for the K-12 education system to educate the volume of highly educated employees that the US economy needs.

Fortunately, the US has many of the world's leading universities. Every year, tens of thousands of students venture huge financial costs and many other risks to study at US universities. Most well-educated and talented graduates stay in the US and contribute significantly to the US economy. In addition, thousands of highly educated foreign employees apply to public authorities to work in the US each year. The country's competitive and productive economy is the most crucial factor in attracting talented and educated foreigners.

However, due to the failure of K-12 education in the US, more and more children of low and middle-income parents are excluded from high-income jobs that require quality education and good academic results. This situation will worsen the deteriorating status of the "middle class" in the medium and long term. Thus, the American education system seems to be based on the assumption that the country's economy can sustain its productivity with high-income students and highly educated immigrants.

This assumption will create economic and political instability in the medium and long term. The American education system is failing its low-income and middle-income students. Increasing the quality of public education is an essential tool for ensuring the continued upward mobility between social classes and the economic and political security of the American middle class.

How education reforms will take shape depends on the implementation of more innovative programs. School choice can play a vital role in the innovative and responsive educational practices necessary to reform the US education system. For this reason, educators, policymakers, and students must be given the freedom they need to generate change.

# References

California Assessment of Student Performance and Progress. (2019). *English language arts/literacy and mathematics: Smart balance summative assessments.* https://caasppelpac.cde.ca.gov/caaspp/DashViewReport?ps=true&lstTestYear=2019&lstTestType=B&lstGroup=1&lstSubGroup=1&lstGrade=8&lstSchoolType=A&lstCounty=00&lstDistrict=0000 0&lstSchool=0000000&lstFocus=a

California Charter School Policy Task Force. (2019). *California Charter School Policy Task Force report submitted June 6, 2019.* California Department of Education. https://www.cde.ca.gov/eo/in/documents/charterstaskforcereport.pdf

California Department of Education. (2021, November 18). *Local control funding formula overview: Information about the funding provisions of the local control funding formula.* https://www.cde.ca.gov/fg/aa/lc/lcffoverview.asp

California Legislative Information. (2019). *AB 1507 charter schools: Location: Resource center.* https://leginfo.legislature.ca.gov/faces/billHistoryClient.xhtml?bill_id=201920200AB1507

California State Auditor. (2019). *K–12 local control funding: The State's approach has not ensured that significant funding is benefiting students as intended to close achievement gaps* (Report No. 2019-101). https://www.auditor.ca.gov/pdfs/reports/2019-101.pdf

Cano, R., & Hong, J. (2022, January 19). *Mind the achievement gap: California's disparities in education, explained.* CalMatters. https://calmatters.org/explainers/achievement-gap-california-explainer-schools-education-disparities-explained/

Center for Research on Education Outcomes. (2013). *National charter school study 2013.* https://credo.stanford.edu/wp-content/uploads/2021/08/ncss_2013_final_draft.pdf

Center for Research on Education Outcomes. (2014). *Charter school performance in California.* https://credo.stanford.edu/wp-content/uploads/2021/08/ca_report_final.pdf

Center for Research on Education Outcomes. (2017, October 4). *CREDO at Stanford University releases New York City charter school study* [Press release]. https://credo.stanford.edu/wp-content/uploads/2021/08/nyc_press_release.pdf

Center for Research on Education Outcomes. (2020, October 22). *CREDO at Stanford University releases updated examination of charter school impacts in Washington state* [Press release]. https://credo.stanford.edu/wp-content/uploads/2021/08/wa_2020_press_release_pdf.pdf

Coulson, A. J. (2009). Comparing public, private, and market schools: The international evidence. *Journal of School Choice, 3*(1), 31–54. https://doi.org/10.1080/15582150902805016

de Brey, C., Musu, L., McFarland, J., Wilkinson-Flicker, S., Diliberti, M., Zhang, A., Branstetter, C., & Wang, X. (2019). *Status and trends in the education of racial and ethnic groups 2018* (NCES Publication No. 2019-038). U.S. Department of Education, National Center for Education Statistics. https://nces.ed.gov/pubs2019/2019038.pdf

De Gregorio, J., & Lee, J.-W. (2002). Education and income inequality: New evidence from cross-country data. *The Review of Income and Wealth, 48*(3), 395–416. https://doi.org/10.1111/1475-4991.00060

Edmark, K., & Persson, L. (2021). The impact of attending an independent upper secondary school: Evidence from Sweden using school ranking data. *Economics of Education Review*, *84*, Article 102148. https://doi.org/10.1016/j.econedurev.2021.102148

Finn, C. E., Jr., Manno, B. V., & Vanourek, G. (2000). *Charter schools in action: Renewing public education*. Princeton University Press.

Forster, G. (2016). *A win-win solution: The empirical evidence on school choice*. Friedman Foundation for Educational Choice. http://www.edchoice.org/wp-content/uploads/2016/05/A-Win-Win-Solution-The-Empirical-Evidence-on-School-Choice.pdf

Friedman, M. (1992). *Capitalism and freedom* (40th anniversary ed.). University of Chicago Press.

Hahnel, C. (2020). *California's education funding crisis explained in 12 charts* [Infographic]. Policy Analysis for California Education. https://edpolicyinca.org/publications/californias-education-funding-crisis-explained-12-charts

Innovate Public Schools. (2019). *2019 top Los Angeles County public schools for underserved students*. https://reports.innovateschools.org/top-la-public-schools/

Kaplan, J. (2017). *Improving but still behind: California's support for K–12 education* [Fact sheet]. California Budget & Policy Center. https://calbudgetcenter.org/resources/improving-but-still-behind-californias-support-for-k-12-education/

Merrifield, J. D., & Gray, N. L. (2013). School choice and development: Evidence from the Edgewood experiment. *Cato Journal*, *33*(1), 127–142.

National Alliance for Public Charter Schools. (2014, August 13). *Separating fact & fiction: What you need to know about public charter schools*. https://www.publiccharters.org/publications/separating-fact-fiction-public-charter-schools

National Center for Education Statistics. (n.d.). *State performance compared to the nation*. The Nation's Report Card. https://www.nationsreportcard.gov/profiles/stateprofile?chort=1&sub=MAT&sj=&sfj=NP&st=MN&year=2019R3

Petek, G. (2020). *Narrowing California's K–12 student achievement gaps*. Legislative Analyst's Office. https://lao.ca.gov/reports/2020/4144/narrowing-k12-gaps-013120.pdf

Sahlgren, G. H. (2010). *Schooling for money: Swedish education reform and the role of the profit motive* (IEA Discussion Paper No. 33). Institute of Economic Affairs. https://www.iea.org.uk/sites/default/files/publications/files/Schooling%20for%20money%20-%20web%20version_0.pdf

Sandström, F. M. (2005). School choice in Sweden: Is there danger of a counterrevolution? In D. Salisbury & J. Tooley (Eds.), *What America can learn from school choice in other countries* (pp. 23–40). Cato Institute.

Shakeel, M. D., Anderson, K. P., & Wolf, P. J. (2016). *The participant effects of private school vouchers across the globe: A meta-analytic and systematic review* (EDRE Working Paper No. 2016-07). University of Arkansas, Department of Education Reform. https://doi.org/10.2139/ssrn.2777633

Sowell, T. (2020). *Charter schools and their enemies*. Basic Books.

Tuttle, C. C., Gill, B., Gleason, P., Knechtel, V., Nichols-Barrer, I., & Resch, A. (2013). *KIPP middle schools: Impacts on achievement and other outcomes* [Executive summary]. Mathematica Policy Research. http://www.kipp.org/wp-content/uploads/2016/09/2013_Mathematica_KIPP_Executive_Summary1.pdf

Ugo, I., & Hill, L. (2017). *Charter schools and California's local control funding formula*. Public Policy Institute of California. https://www.ppic.org/wp-content/uploads/r_0917iur.pdf

van Ewijk, R., & Sleegers, P. (2010). The effect of peer socioeconomic status on student achievement: A meta-analysis. *Educational Research Review*, *5*(2), 134–150. https://doi.org/10.1016/j.edurev.2010.02.001

van Ham, M., Hedman, L., Manley, D., Coulter, R., & Östh, J. (2014). Intergenerational transmission of neighbourhood poverty: An analysis of neighbourhood histories of individuals. *Transactions of the Institute of British Geographers*, *39*(3), 402–417. https://doi.org/10.1111/tran.12040

Veney, D., & Jacobs, D. (2021). *Voting with their feet: A state-level analysis of public charter school and district public school trends*. National Alliance for Public Charter Schools. https://www.publiccharters.org/sites/default/files/documents/2021-09/napcs_voting_feet_rd6.pdf

Walberg, H. J. (2007). *School choice: The findings*. Cato Institute.

White, J., & Hieronimus, M. (2022, February 9). *1. How many charter schools and students are there?* data.publiccharters.org. https://data.publiccharters.org/digest/charter-school-data-digest/how-many-charter-schools-and-students-are-there/

World Population Review. (n.d.). *High school graduation rates by state 2022*. https://worldpopulationreview.com/state-rankings/high-school-graduation-rates-by-state

# The housing market in California: problems with its function and tentative suggestions for reform.

# The housing market in California: problems with its function and tentative suggestions for reform.

## Abstract

D ue to tremendous price growth in many urban areas, home affordability is major political issue in California. In this chapter, we examine some of the economic drivers of this phenomenon, and find that the basic cause for rising California housing prices is the state's increasingly strict zoning and other land-use regulations. As a result of poorly functioning housing markets, regional labor markets are impeded, the environment is damaged, and low and moderate income families are deprived of economic opportunity. Building a regulatory framework that strikes a balance between economic growth, home affordability, and development sustainability while simultaneously safeguarding the environment is the answer to California's housing affordability challenge. At the same time, it is vital to protect California's distinctive historical legacy while also developing a growth strategy that addresses traffic congestion and rising public utility costs. More housing, especially multifamily housing units, is needed, and this may be done while taking other concerns into mind. We argue for a more reasonable amount of state intervention in the housing market, and discuss the types of policy tools that state policymakers can use to influence housing market outcomes.

# 1. Introduction

In recent years, housing affordability has become a major political problem in California because of the significant price growth in many urban regions. At the state level, housing prices have risen faster than inflation for last two decades (Figure 1). In spite of having only 12 percent of the US population, California today has 27 percent of the country's homeless.[1] In terms of home affordability, California is rated forty-ninth.

Although local governments have generally been in charge of land use management and housing development, there are compelling economic reasons for limiting local government participation. It is our contention that policymakers in California ought to consider a more

---

[1] By way of comparison, as the only other state to surpass the five-percent mark, New York, has a rate of 16 percent of individuals who are chronically homeless.

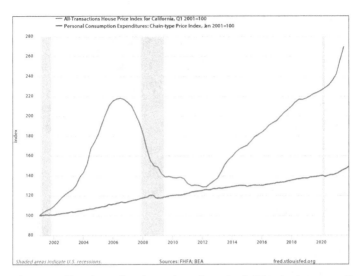

Figure 1: Housing prices have risen faster in California than overall inflation. 1st Jan 2001 to 1st Nov 2021. Estimated using sales prices and appraisal data.

sensible level of intensity of state involvement in the housing market, and reach for the sort of free-market policy tools that will help achieve more coherent objectives and market outcomes.

The rest of the chapter is organised as follows. In section 2 we discuss the issues related to restrictive zoning, which has a direct impact on the cost of housing in California. Here we rely on some of the most relevant empirical studies; for example, according to one influential study restrictive zoning regulations increased San Francisco and San Jose's housing prices by approximately 50 percent. In section 3 we discuss how the incentives and behavior of market participants – families, local and municipal governments, developers, landlords, and so on – will be affected by any new legislation. As a cautionary example, the California Environmental Quality Act (CEQA) is used to show how a law that was intended to mitigate the deleterious effects of climate damage may instead be used as a weapon to thwart socially advantageous infrastructure projects. Other examples of policy overlap are cited. Section 4 discusses housing's importance to the wider economy. Section 5 provides a comprehensive discussion of rent controls, extending the straightforward supply-and-demand logic of previous sections into supporting theoretical arguments. Section 6 concludes with tentative recommendations for policy.

## 2. Restrictive zoning

In this section we discuss the issues related to restrictive zoning, which has a direct impact on the cost of housing in California. According to Glaeser et al 2005's study, restrictive zoning regulations increased San Francisco and San Jose's housing prices by about 50 percent. Today, this premium is even higher (see [10] for a summary of recent evidence). Similar results have been found in other studies [57], which share a common conclusion: it is difficult to build new housing units and public infrastructure because of zoning regulations. There is a significant barrier to constructing new housing in California because 66–80 percent of all properties are designated for single-family residences. This, in turn, prevents the construction of high-density housing, which could save precious urban land. As Furth and Gonzalez [30] argue,

*strict zoning restricts human freedom, increases rent, and decreases housing supply to degrees that make it worthy of public concern.*

According to a 2018 survey by the Terner Center for Housing Innovation at the University of California, Berkeley, 94 percent of residential land in San Jose is zoned for single-family homes. Single-family housing can account for 60 percent or more of the residential zoning in some of the large metro areas like Los Angeles. At least 95 percent of the land in Atherton, a wealthy Bay Area town, is set aside for single-family homes. Overall, about 80 percent of the homes in the state's residential areas are single-family dwellings. High-density housing, which can save money on scarce urban land, is prevented as a result. Single-family homes are no longer an option if California's housing market is to become more affordable.

Recently, we have witnessed increasing interest in using state legislation to circumvent local zoning rules and alter single-family zoned areas. As a result of California Senate Bill 35, which was passed in 2017, local governments and counties that failed to meet the number of housing units assigned to them by the regional planning authority were subject to a ministerial approval process. It restricts the number of times local governments must review projects, thereby streamlining the approval process, and it exempts qualified projects from California Environmental Quality Act (CEQA) review by using a ministerial rather than a discretionary approval process.

The success of this policy change has been modest since there have been relatively few successful applications [55]. There could be a number of reasons for this lack of successful applications. Because ministerial permission does not ensure development, opponents may sue after a project is approved (or is not halted), claiming that it does not qualify for ministerial approval. SB 35 also has the downside of requiring that a significant portion of a development be set aside for housing at prices below market rate. The cost of building a home is further increased by the need for builders to pay prevailing wages, which may be rather high. Joint requirements diminish or muddle incentives to construct since the cost savings resulting in expedited approval are compensated by higher salaries and lower revenue from requiring a significant number of units to be held aside at below-market rates.

Similarly, a number of proposals have been filed in the state assembly to rezone single-family neighborhoods to accommodate multifamily dwellings as well as apartments. Despite this, these reforms have not yet been implemented, likely because of the considerable political pressure exerted against them by opponents. For example, "fourplexes" in single-family communities could have been authorized under Senate Bill 50, which could also have allowed five-story constructions at transit hubs and in job-rich regions. Splitting the two parts of SB 50 into two different bills, allowing duplexes and/or triplexes in single-family sites, and addressing the more-controversial issue of highly dense housing around transit stations or job-rich regions, might be a more viable answer.

It may be beneficial to look to other states for analogous scenarios and lessons arising from such. For example, duplex and triplex legislation has been successfully established in single-family areas in Oregon. More local buy-in might make this easier in California, reducing political pressure on lawmakers to stop the move. Duplex and triplex units fit more readily into a single-family home's constructed environment than bigger apartment complexes, therefore opponents of SB 50 would be denied one of their greatest arguments by separating them from the more problematic multifamily portion of the bill. SB 1120, which would have permitted duplexes in single-family zones in 2020, was defeated by the state Senate. In order to meet the legislative deadline, the state's lower house, the assembly, brought up the measure for a vote with little time remaining.

The conversion of industrial, retail, and commercial buildings into residential and mixed-use space would be a simpler zoning change to achieve. It is no accident that the COVID-19 epidemic has accelerated trends that were already under way, such as the shrinking need for certain commercial places (e.g. malls), and the increased mobility of jobs due to the rise of work done at home or elsewhere. As time goes on, this might serve as a valuable new source of housing supply, thus state and local officials should make it a top priority to implement this measure. In areas now classified for commercial or industrial use, allowing residential development would be a reasonable solution, unless there are urgent health, safety, or environmental concerns that would prevent the construction of new homes. As we emerge from the epidemic, there is considerable debate over whether or not transforming offices and retail centers into flats would be cost-effective. A more comprehensive approach would be to let the market resolve these concerns instead of prohibiting the use of this area for residential purposes via zoning restrictions.

## 3. Policy overlap and unintended consequences: some illustrative examples

### 3.1. CEQA

The incentives and behavior of market participants – families, local and municipal governments, developers, landlords, and so on – will be affected by any new legislation. As a cautionary tale, the California Environmental Quality Act (CEQA) shows how a law that was intended to mitigate the deleterious effects of climate damage may instead be used as a weapon to thwart climate-friendly infrastructure projects. In some circumstances, midcourse corrections may be made by monitoring policy results, including any spillovers across geographic regions or policy sectors. However, it it tends to be difficult to undo the damage done by bad policies once they have become entrenched.

The National Environmental Protection Act was established by Congress in 1969. Projects having negative environmental impacts may still go ahead under this law, but they must be made public beforehand. But the criteria of CEQA, which was approved in 1970, are significantly more stringent. CEQA, unlike its predecessor, mandates that state and local governments avoid projects that harm the environment to the greatest degree feasible.

In order to proceed with a project that will have a detrimental impact on the environment, CEQA requires that harm be minimized; projects may be rejected if a more environmentally friendly option is available. CEQA mandates that the permitting bodies (state and/or local government agencies) increase public engagement in the process and permits private parties to file lawsuits. CEQA is plagued by two serious weaknesses that compound one other's effects. Environmental mitigation without cost-benefit analysis is one of the requirements. Private law-suits, on the other hand, are completely unchecked. Both of these scenarios may result in a wildly inefficient alloca-tion of resources.

Economic inefficiency is an obvious and direct result of the first scenario. Understanding the advantages and costs of using a certain resource is essential to any choice on how to allocate those resources. The environmental effect of any development must be balanced against the advantages of the mitigation effort if the project is to be efficient. The cost benefit analysis approach should guide any debate on these matters, even if there is fair disagreement. Spending millions of dollars on mitigation for a project with environmental benefits that are a fraction of that amount is a waste of public money.

California has a wide range of state legislation aimed at protecting the environment, but the effects on land use and housing construction patterns are particularly complex. As the first state legislation of its type, the California Environmental Quality Act (CEQA) aimed to alert policymakers and the public about negative environmental repercussions of large projects. Since its inception, CEQA has come under fire for its open-ended character, which allows opponents of new development to delay or block even environmentally-friendly initiatives [17]. Many new housing developments have been built close to public transit in fire and flood-prone regions in California since the implementation of CEQA in the 1970s, despite the fact that total production has been unable to keep pace with demand [18].

It is clear that CEQA has achieved many good environmental aims, but it has also been misused. There are a number of organizations that are using CEQA lawsuits to delay or stop construction for reasons that have nothing to do with environmental concerns. Hernandez et al [40] provide a number of convincing arguments to this effect. Nearly half of the CEQA lawsuits, according to the authors, is aimed at public programs with no connection to private commercial interests, such as initiatives to help people minimize their carbon footprints. An infill development project (a redevelopment of previously developed regions inside a city or municipality) accounts for 80 percent of the contested agency approvals for projects having a particular physical location. Infill housing construction was originally meant to be exempt from CEQA, but only a small number of projects have taken advantage of this exemption [12].

So what can be done? Reforming the CEQA is a critical first step. While CEQA has helped to achieve a number of important environmental goals, it is also being exploited in ways that were not intended. CEQA lawsuits, in particular, are routinely employed by groups seeking to delay or prevent development for a number of reasons, many of which have nothing to do with environmental concerns. Nearly half of CEQA litigation focuses on public projects that are unrelated to private business interests, and 80 percent of challenged agency approvals of projects with a specific physical location are infill development projects (i.e., projects that redevelop already existing areas within cities and townships).

Furthermore, corporations that wish to keep rivals out of their markets and labour unions that want to improve their bargaining leverage against both public and private employers use CEQA litigation. Overall, about half of CEQA litigation are resolved in the plaintiff's favour, thus incentivizing individuals who file CEQA-related lawsuits. Some of the biggest abuses of CEQA litigation might be remedied with a few easy and commonsense modifications. First and foremost, duplicative litigation should be avoided, especially for projects that have already passed CEQA scrutiny. Then, procedural improvements should make it illegal to use delaying tactics.

Moreover, as is the case in other civil lawsuits, losing parties in CEQA legislation should pay for court costs and attorney's fees. Exceptions to this regulation could only be made in exceptional situations. Judicial remedies, particularly for minor flaws, should be restricted to resolving those issues rather than rescinding a public agency's project approval and forcing a CEQA re-evaluation. All litigants should be required to adhere to severe disclosure regulations regarding their names and interests. The guidelines would prevent non-environmental goals from being concealed beneath appealing, environmentally oriented labels.

Last but not least, historical preservation requirements should be strengthened to guarantee that only really significant buildings are saved, rather than just ancient structures with little historical or architectural significance.

## 3.2. UGBs and LAFCOs

The populations of Southern California, the San Francisco Bay Area, and the Sacramento region make up the bulk of the state's total population. Other than the coastal regions previously referenced, much of California is sparsely inhabited. Developing areas outside of main population centers should be included in the process of increasing California's housing supply. This is not least because NIMBYism in densely populated places creates significant obstacles to new construction, which are not present in less densely populated areas. "Urban Growth Boundaries" which are government-established boundaries that divide urban areas from agricultural and/or undeveloped regions, will have to be reformed to accomplish this.

Typically, these limits are authorized by the public and remain in place for a predetermined amount of time. In the 1990s, the San Francisco Bay Area was the first area to have a UGB. The primary goal of these limitations is to prevent urban expansion in greenbelt regions. The impact they have is comparable to that of "Local Agency Formation Commissions" (LAFCOs), regional planning commissions established under California law to limit growth. There are some cases in which a binding UGB can hinder development even when the LAFCO objections are eased, which is troubling because they are often used in conjunction. It is becoming increasingly difficult for certain cities to expand since they have already exceeded their UGBs [59].

UGBs drive up house costs by regulating how land may be utilized and preventing land from being assigned to its highest-valued use, hence raising the price of land in urban areas. One of the most essential reforms is to increase the borders and redistribute land now used for farming to housing. Currently, around 43 percent of California's land is used for agricultural purposes, so even a minor reallocation might make a significant impact in the quantity of land available for housing [60].

There is a case to address LAFCOs and UGB restrictions, which have a major influence on how a city or metropolitan area may expand, limit the quantity of land that can be used to build new homes. Agricultural property could be converted to urban development, multifamily housing must be introduced into single-family home zones, and commercial, industrial, and retail space could be transformed into residential and mixed-use development.

## 4. Wider implications

From the arguments above we can infer that that if serious changes are not implemented, the housing crisis in California will intensify and the gap between the relatively well-off and the poor will increase. Families with school-aged children, especially those in the middle of the economic spectrum, will move out of California, leaving the state mostly to wealthy families able to bear the state's relatively high housing costs; as is shown in Figure 2, California has the second-highest rental prices, surpassed only by Hawaii (note that nearly half of California's residents live in rentals). Household wages in California do not even come close to matching these enormously high housing costs. Housing affordability is critical for a state's people' well-being, especially for low and moderate-income households. The most rigorous zoning regulations apply to small, dense kinds of housing, such as apartments, which are more likely to be used as rental housing.

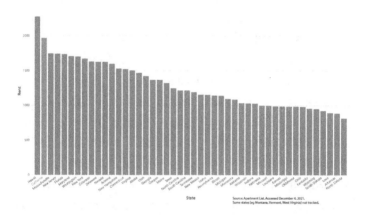

Figure 2: Where are the highest rents?

This is because the bulk of state's high-paying occupations can be found in these places, and the demand for homes in these areas is considerable. Due to a lack of new housing supply, growing demand drives up prices, wiping out any profits made by living and working in these locations. As a consequence, many Californians work in coastal locations, but choose to live elsewhere in the state where housing is less expensive. The majority of Californians who do not already own equity in their homes may never be able to afford a home unless these challenges are solved. But what does it mean for the economy? Let us now examine this further.

## 4.1. The importance of the housing sector to the wider economy

Housing's importance to the economy cannot be overstated. It is the most valuable component of household finance as well as the most important source of consumer spending. The output of the housing sector has a significant impact on both the macroeconomic cycle and employment. Due to the considerable costs associated with residential mobility, housing is a basic requirement that cannot be easily changed. Because of the influence of housing standards on health and educational performance, understanding housing market dynamics is crucial for solving major social problems such as inequality of opportunity. Furthermore, fundamental or policy-induced changes in property values may have large distributional repercussions for owners and tenants across generations.

The empirically documented rise in real estate prices in the United States during the last three decades is in sharp contrast to previously observed historical patterns.[2] Despite the fact that housebuilding is a fairly

[2] See Cournede et al. [13] for a discussion.

dynamic sector with minimal inherent barriers to entry, recent demand in United States consistently exceeds supply, leading prices to increase to levels that are often unaffordable. It is not surprising, therefore, that the rise in inflation adjusted housing prices has sparked heated policy debates about the potential negative consequences of increased rents on economic growth.

Increasing costs may have a negative impact on the economy in a variety of ways. Rising housing prices, for example, may limit the economy's development potential by discouraging potential migrants, changing the labor market's growth balance from employment to wages, and lowering competitiveness. In many industrialised nations, real property prices climbed in lockstep or slightly behind actual building costs during the millennium and the first part of the twentieth century. For at least two reasons, these patterns are worthy of observation. For starters, they occurred during a time when many countries were short on labor and resources as a result of wartime losses and destruction. Second, they happened despite significant gains in housing efficiency at the time, when many residences were connected to sanitary, sewage, and power networks.

Housing-related policy measures have a significant effect on the economy's overall productivity. For example, there is substantial evidence that restricting mortgage interest deductions lowers property rates, decreases housing supply, increases homeownership, reduces mortgage debt, and boosts welfare [58, 1]. Data also suggests that a lower marginal effective tax rate on residential land, which is typically the consequence of increased mortgage interest deductions, increases the income elasticity of house prices. Reduced income tax incentives for home purchases, according to this line of research, has the benefit of reducing the impact of increased demand on house prices [11].

Land-use control policies matter. A high degree of decentralisation of land-use options is empirically associated with high rigidity of housing supply [9, 11]. In this context, the reader may be familiar with the so-called home-voter theory, first proposed by land-use economist William Fischel, which suggests that homeowners would lobby local politicians to protect the integrity of their property investment by restricting land development [26, 37]. When many tiers of government veto projects and political economy tensions escalate, responsibility overlaps are correlated with project delays [38].

Market rules also matter. Tight rental market rules have been found to impede residential expansion by reducing incentives to invest in rental housing. This is due to lower rental earnings and increased difficulty in selling real estate assets caused by tight occupancy requirements [43]. This is backed by studies where researchers have found that rent regulation in San Francisco limits housing availability by as much as 15 percent [16]. Moreover, there is evidence that in the case of strict rental sector control, the house price elasticity of residential development is significantly smaller [11]. Higher housing prices and lower availability, in the long run, obstruct access to home ownership, further boosting both rents and home prices. Hence, imposition of rent controls is likely to outweigh the short-term gains for rent-paying low-income families. Worse, there is evidence that tight rent control tends to intensify speculative bubbles, leading to heightened economic uncertainty [13].

Apart from economic considerations, the housing market is ripe for analysis from a geospatial perspective. Natural and man-made housing supply constraints, which are either rarely regulated or not relevant to regulation, can have an equally profound impact on the effective functioning of housing markets. Supply elasticity may, in fact, be hampered by geographical constraints.

Geographical considerations matter not least because economic activity tends to be unevenly distributed over space, as evidenced by the development of cities and the concentration of economic functions in certain locations within cities. Even the most casual observer should be able to see how the intensity of the agglomeration and dispersion processes that support these concentrations of economic activity affects a number of social and commercial activities. The delicate equilibrium between these two sets of forces has an impact on areas such as expenditure growth, city-level and national-level efficiency, and factor wages both mobile and immobile, among others. The effect of place-based policies, such as transportation infrastructure investments, municipal taxation, and land management, heavily determines the equilibrium between these forces.

These broad economic principles tend to be widely accepted and uncontroversial. However, there is considerable scope for discussion when it comes to policy prescription. In fact, where policymakers tend to differ is the degree of control over housing creation by the state and local government.

## 4.2. What policy instruments are available?

Taxes, subsidies, regulations, and information sharing are just some of the instruments that state and local governments use to impact housing supply and affordability. As a foundation for local governance, state governments define and delegate monetary power and land-use jurisdiction, among other things. For each level of government, Table 1 tabulates a summary of some of the most important policy instruments.

| Policy type | State | Local |
|---|---|---|
| Regulations | Set parameters for local govt zoning authority (enabling legislation) | Write & enforce zoning, historic preservation |
| | Environmental regulations (above natl baseline) | Enforce building code, fire safety |
| | State minimum wage (above federal) | Local minimum wages |
| | Occupational & business licensing (e.g. real estate agents, mortgage brokers, building trades) | Adjudicate landlord-tenant disputes (evictions) |
| | Regulate landlord-tenant relationships | |
| | Some regional planning requirements | |
| Taxes | Set parameters for local govt fiscal authority (TEL) | Set & administer property taxes Municipal bonds (long-term infrastructure, subsidized hsg) |

| Subsidies | Some housing construction & maintenance (rehab & weatherization grants) | Local housing trust funds, rental assistance (incl impact fees, & other exactions e.g. IZ) |
| --- | --- | --- |
| | Distribute federal grants (LIHTC, CDBG, transit) | Homebuyer assistance programs |
| | Grants to localities for housing-related infrastructure (schools, transportation) | Administer state & federal subsidies (vouchers, public housing, CDBG) |
| Information sharing | Some research & technical assistance | Maintain property records |
| | Set requirements for information disclosure (e.g. sales transactions) | |

Table 1: Multiple policy levers are at the disposal of state and local governments when it comes to housing supply. Source: Schuetz (2022) [59]

Land use regulation is a governmental responsibility that has been delegated by states to local governments. Cities and counties in different states are given varying amounts of policy headroom by their respective state governments. State governments have the capacity to revoke authority since it begins with them. Pre-empting certain instruments or actions is one of the less common ways to limit local governments' hands. For example, almost half of states ban municipal price control measures for rental accommodation.

A variety of indirect avenues are also available for states to control housing. States all around the country have implemented environmental protection rules that go above the federal minimum (as defined by the National Environmental Protection Act), requiring extra review procedures that might slow or halt construction. Most states have adopted or not enacted building regulations that control the health and safety of all buildings; other states have implemented stricter energy efficiency require- ments, raising initial construction costs while reducing long-term energy consumption. The labor component of building expenses is influenced by state and union mini- mum wage rules and work restrictions. Real estate agents, appraisers, and mortgage brokers are subject to occupa- tional and business licensing laws that impact the trans- action costs of buying and selling property. In addition, state governments control the legal framework for land- lord-tenant interactions, including how leases and evic- tion processes may be structured.

Although zoning rules are the most frequently studied and generally implemented type of housing control, local governments also utilize a broad variety of other measures. In addition to federal and state minimums, local environmental laws, fire safety, and subdivision regulations all have an impact on the cost and viability of new construction. When implementing statewide legislation, like as health standards and seismic restrictions, local authorities frequently have the option of deviating from them.

Compared to other consumer products and services, the level of local control over housing production is exceptional. The localized expenses of house building often justify this. Expanding a community's housing stock increases the need for public services like schools and roads while also decreasing the quality of life for existing inhabitants (increased noise or traffic congestion). Local governments have both financial and political constraints to limit the construction of low-cost housing in their territories because of these concentrated negative consequences of new development.

Transportation, schools, crime prevention, and water infrastructure all fall within the purview of local governments, who are ultimately responsible for supporting them. The need for these services grows as more housing is created in a city or county. The money generated by property taxes, impact fees, and other methods is an essential issue for local governments when restricting development. It is not an uncommon belief amongst local authorities that the construction of more modest, lower-cost dwellings would have a negative impact on the local economy that has led to zoning laws such as apartment bans and big minimum lot sizes [27, 36]. This appears to be a widely held belief, however it is difficult to measure the true financial effect of new construction.

Pressure from the public is also exerted on local elected authorities to prevent new house building, particularly in the moderate-priced ranges. It is very uncommon for residents to protest any changes that they perceive would decrease property prices or affect the nature of their area. Existing homeowners now have a great deal of authority to halt unwelcome development, thanks to changes in the development process during the last three decades [15, 18]. Though it comes to approving development plans, older, richer homeowners tend to predominate, even when they are just a minority of the local population [21, 48].

On the political and budgetary fronts, local governments' adoption of very restrictive zoning that restricts the amount of new construction and authorizes only expensive new residences is not entirely unexpected. However, it should not be a surprise that excessively stringent municipal housing regulations may have a negative impact on regional and state housing markets. Excessive municipal zoning and land use laws have been shown to reduce the amount of housing built in high-demand areas and increase the cost of housing, compared to less tightly controlled markets.

As a result of poorly functioning housing markets, regional labor markets are impeded, the environment is damaged, and low and moderate-income families are deprived of economic opportunity. Regulations that restrict the construction of new homes and raise their prices have far-reaching effects on the whole country's economy. A 36 percent loss in GDP is estimated to have occurred in the United States between 1964 and 2009 – directly attributable to restrictive land use regulations [41].

It is more difficult for companies in costly areas to recruit and retain employees, who want higher salaries to cover the cost of living. Some potential employees are reluctant to relocate to high-productivity locations because of the significant rise in housing expenses in urban cities like San Francisco [32]. Most new homes are constructed on the outskirts of cities, distant from employment areas and public transit, which leads to lengthier commutes and increased traffic [14].

Last but not least, climate change and resource use are directly linked to the spatial patterns of home growth. Suburban residents have higher carbon footprints than their urban counterparts, mostly due to disparities in housing consumption and transportation [35, 42]. Infill development – increasing population density around urban cores and public transportation – can arguably accommodate population and employment expansion at the state level while causing less environmental damage.

# 5. Who benefits from rent controls?

Landlords are subject to rent controls in a dozen California communities, including Berkeley, Beverly Hills, East Palo Alto, Hayward, Los Angeles, Los Gatos, Oakland, Palm Springs, San Francisco, San Jose, Santa Monica, and West Hollywood. In what follows, we review the available instruments of government engagement in the residential rental sector and argue that, unlike most public policies, the legitimacy of rent control is seriously in question. We first examine rent controls in their historical context and proceed to provide a basic theoretical framework for rent caps as instruments of government engagement in the residential rental sector.

## 5.1. Rent controls in their historical context

On numerous occasions, the need for intervention in the residential rental market has been justified by the need for macro-financial stability. The scarcity of rental accommodation, in particular, is a barrier to the labor market's efficient functioning because it hinders employee mobility, particularly among younger workers. As a result, if working-class households occupied a higher proportion of rental property than owner-occupied housing, it would be easier for unemployed people to relocate to locations where new job possibilities are established or where jobs are available. Rent increases in some households can have a big impact on macroeconomic stability, especially if they are concentrated among people who do not save much and are more likely to consume. Changes in rent lower demand for other products in these households' shopping baskets, thereby increasing the number of households whose consumption is limited by their present income level.

As a result of this shift in the composition of household consumption, aggregate demand and economic activity may be more exposed to future cyclical fluctuations. Furthermore, in a low-yielding capital asset market, residential rental investments may be more appealing, which could have implications for the economy's financial stability. It is the link between house prices and returns on investment in residential rentals that creates this macrofinancial risk. Indeed, providing incentives to invest in real assets, such as affordable housing, will drive up property prices and, in turn, increase mortgage credit.

In light of this, we will now seek, based on widely accepted principles of public policy, to assess the fundamental tools of government participation in the residential rental sector. Government-induced incentives relating to the construction of affordable housing, rent limits, and a wide range of heterogeneous measures aimed at both incentivizing the availability of private residential accommodation and containing the increase in rent expenditure faced by certain groups are the three main types of policies. This examination of international practice and discussion of policy implications is not intended to be exhaustive, but rather to highlight the most significant policies in advanced economies. The immediate goal is to highlight the difficulties of implementing residential rental assistance programs, as well as the potential benefits and drawbacks of various approaches.

It is crucial to recognize, however, the limitations of applying lessons from earlier experience in widely diverse regional marketplaces to the current situation. Although general conclusions can be drawn in a variety of situations, the effectiveness of residential rental market policies is determined by their interaction with the macroeconomic situation, local housing market factors, and, in general, a wide range of other policies that affect the housing market's functioning – such as tax or labor market policies – as well as the income dynamics of households seeking rented housing.

Government involvement in the form of residential rent caps is one example. Residential rent caps appear to provide an immediate solution to the casual observer. They provide a technique to mitigate the negative effects of rising rental costs on household well-being without incurring a significant financial outlay. The most prevalent argument given for such limits in places where rental prices are fast growing is the need to ensure that families, particularly lower-income households, have access to affordable housing. Only in exceptional instances, such as after World Wars, during times of crisis, or in reaction to abrupt changes in residential housing rates in large cities with strong population growth and short-term supply rigidities in the rental sector, have rent restrictions been introduced.

Rent controls were enacted in a number of European countries during the First World War. They were first used in the United States shortly after the country's entry into World War II. In both cases, the war effort compelled a large portion of the population to relocate, putting upward pressure on residential rental prices in locations where economic activity was concentrated. Nominal rentals were suspended as a transitory measure to ensure stability, affecting the majority of the available housing stock. As troops returned to the major cities in the United States as the Second World War began, these limitations remained in effect. With the exception of New York City, they were eventually lifted towards the end of the 1940s. Residential rent caps and varying degrees of rental housing stock coverage were in place in Europe until the 1980s, when the majority of the housing stock was demolished following WWII and had to be rebuilt.

There are two types of rent control measures that are typically used: first-generation and second-generation. The first generation of rent controls refers to the widespread practice in industrialized countries of imposing rent controls on a significant section of the housing sector, which are typically implemented by central governments. Because these regulations tended to affect older housing stock, dual residential rent markets emerged, in which controlled residential rental rates fell in real terms while prices in the unregulated new residential rental sector segment eventually rose.

The 1970s saw the emergence of the second generation of rent controls. These limitations, which are frequently tied to a cost-of-living metric such as the consumer price index, keep rental price increases in check. As a result, during periods of escalating depression, such as the oil shocks of the 1970s, actual rental rates became set. This sort of rent restriction was implemented in a wide number of sophisticated economies, while policy designs varied greatly. The initiatives comprised a wide range of upgrade laws and measures, including procedures that limit rental price growth but do not include rent freezes per se. In some countries and localities, rent adjustments were related to the leased property rather than the individual. In some cases, landlords were reimbursed for increased maintenance costs, while in others, fixed minimum rates of return were included.

Furthermore, the requirements remained to apply to present housing stock, but not to rentals built after the regulations went into effect. Over time, rent ceilings have grown to cover the portion of the housing stock that was initially omitted in some jurisdictions. Market caps were first adopted – both in major Californian cities such as San Francisco, Los Angeles, as well as nationally (including Boston and Washington, D.C.) – in response to large increases in residential rental prices, but they have subsequently spread to other economies, albeit in various ways.

Analogous measures that have been passed in the United States are also of relevance. These were enacted to limit the rise in residential rental costs in cities and states that had been affected by rising rents or had further housing access difficulties. The new rent restrictions often impose limits on the growth of rental prices. Individual property markets provide a wide range of regulations, each with its own set of features, but in general, rent controls are used to keep rental price inflation in check. These regulatory ceilings are greater than the consumer price index, which allows for actual rent growth. Furthermore, the limits apply to current rental contracts, and usually only apartments in multi-family housing above a particular age are affected. Price limitations apply to the bulk of the residential rental market in certain circumstances, with exceptions for a few extremely specific categories of housing, and the restrictions apply to the rented homes rather than the residents. Rent increases in California, for example, are capped at 5 per cent per year plus inflation beginning in 2020 and lasting ten years. With the exception of single-family residences maintained by minor landlords, the regulation applies to properties built more than 15 years ago. The age or volume of residential buildings, whether managed by companies or retail owners, has no bearing on rent limitations. By comparison, the restrictions in Oregon, which cap yearly rental rate increases at the consumer price index +7 percent, apply to the whole rental industry. These state laws are usually in line with city ordinances. For example, in the city of Los Angeles, rent increases are limited to between 3 percent and 4 percent for housing units built before October 1978 that are not single-family houses, whereas rent increases in San Jose are limited to 5 percent each year.

These rules limit the amount of rent that can be charged in older homes. They have set maximum rent increases based on lease term, as well as maximum rental increases when a tenant moves out and the property is improved. These requirements apply to any structures with six or more housing units built between 1947 and 1973. The constraints on residential price fluctuations are still extended when there is a shift in occupier in home that was previously subject to market restrictions. These rent-control measures were believed to effect about one million housing units, or over half of the city's residential rental market. According to a report from the NYU Furman Center for Real Estate and Urban Policy [29], controlled rents in Manhattan in 2011 were 75 percent of the usual free-market rent per month (50 percent).

General price controls, or price caps on a wide range of items, are frequently implemented in response to public concerns about out-of-control inflation. Throughout the twentieth century, the threat of war was frequently used to justify the imposition of broad price controls. In this case, one could argue that the psychological benefits of rules outweigh the costs of shortages, illegal markets, and rationing, at least in the short term. Inflationary pressures can lead to panic buying, protests, and animosity toward racial or ethnic minorities perceived to benefit from inflation. Price controls can help alleviate these concerns, especially if patriotism is used as a deterrent to tax evasion. Those benefits, however, are unlikely to last for the duration of the conflict.

Furthermore, even during times of war, the majority of inflation is caused by inflationary monetary and fiscal policies, not by panic buying. To the degree that wartime caps curb price rises caused by monetary and fiscal policies, they merely delay the inevitable, transforming what would have been an era of stable inflation into one of sluggish inflation accompanied by more severe inflation. Additionally, some of the perceived resilience of price indexes during warfare is an illusion. Many of the difficulties associated with price controls—queuing, evasion, black markets, and rationing—increase the actual price of commodities for buyers, and these consequences are only partially accounted for as price indexes are measured. When sanctions are lifted, latent inflation becomes visible. For example, estimated inflation remained relatively low during World War II. However, after sanctions were abolished, the consumer price index increased 18 per cent between December 1945 and December 1946, the largest one-year surge in this century.

Inflation is exceedingly difficult to curb by broad-based restrictions, in part because certain costs are invariably left unregulated. At times, the omission of such prices is intentional. The rationale for regulating only a subset of prices—say, that of steel, wheat, and oil—is that these commodities are strategic in the sense that controlling their prices is necessary to stabilise the overall price trend. However, demand continues to move from the regulated to the unregulated market, causing the latter's prices to increase much higher than before. Resources seem to obey costs, and suppliers throughout the unregulated market appear to increase at the cost of resources in the regulated sector. Since the regulated sector was initially selected to cover products considered to be critical inputs for a variety of manufacturing processes, the decrease in the quantity of these inputs is especially vexing. Thus, if controls are maintained for an extended period of time, a government that starts by regulating rates on specific commodities is likely to replace them with broad-based controls. This is precisely what occurred in the United States after WWII.

A second challenge with broad price restrictions is the trade-off between the need for a well-defined program that is widely regarded as fair and the need for sufficient flexibility to maintain a performance appearance. While keeping the majority of prices steady is necessary for simplicity, productivity needs regular modifications. Relative cost adjustments, on the other hand, expose the controls bureaucracy to a storm of lobbying and unfairness claims.

The American experience during World War II brought this struggle to a head. Initially, relative prices were adjusted, often on economists' recommendations, in order to remove possible shortages and other distortions in real markets. However, mounting concerns that the scheme was unjust and was failing to contain inflation prompted President Roosevelt to deliver his controversial 'hold-the-line' order in April 1943, freezing the majority of costs. Regardless of its economic shortcomings, the hold-the-line order was simple to justify and promote to the public.

The argument for general controls during peacetime is based on the possibility that controls will help smooth the transition from high to low inflation. If, after a prolonged period of inflation, a tight money policy is implemented to rein in inflation, some prices will continue to grow at their previous higher rate for a while. Wages, in particular, can continue to increase as a result of long-term contracts or because employees are unaware of the magnitude of the policy reform. This results in increased unemployment and decreased productivity. Price controls may help to contain these disinflationary costs by banning wage rises that are out of step with new demand and price patterns. From this vantage point, conservative monetary policy is the procedure that cures inflation, while market and wage caps provide only short term relief for the suffering.

Although the argument is always rational, the outcome is often not. Price caps, in the eyes of the electorate, absolve the monetary authority of blame for inflation. As a consequence, a Central Bank's pressure to avoid recession may result in the continuation or even acceleration of unsustainable money supply expansion. The analgesic is confused with the antidote.

Price caps offer critical economic insight. By analysing instances in which price mechanisms have been rendered ineffective, we may obtain a greater respect for their inherent beauty and effectiveness. This is not to say that interim controls are ineffective in all situations. However, a careful reading of economic history demonstrates how uncommon these conditions are.

There is a vast economic literature, which almost universally rejects rent controls, even in their more versatile iterations, considering them ineffective tools for combating the consequences of housing market shortages [5, 35]. Research suggests that rent caps result in immediate decreases in the market value of residential housing [19, 24, 49], adversely affect refurbishment, reduce maintenance [45, 3, 56, 54], suppress construction activity [51, 35], and induce inefficient unit allocation [34, 35], all while having ambiguous effects in the short run. Moreover, the targeted groups only benefit in part [47, 6, 34]. Some of of these findings are based on theoretical models that provide, at best, vague forecasts on the consequences of rent controls, depending on the viability of the hypotheses. This has not escaped scholarly critique [4, 56, 45]. However, empirical evidence tends to suggest that adverse or unintended effects of rent controls prices are likely to occur, and that there are no consistent benefits to tenants (see e.g. [19, 20], or [62] for a survey). Research examining the recent introduction of rent controls in United states suggests that tenancy rent regulation decreased family mobility, reduced the size of the residential housing estate, and was a driver of rent inflation across the region [16, 63]. Empirical research on the introduction of rent controls in Germany have shown distorting or adverse effects on the market [61, 52]. Such finding tend to be supported by long-run data on both rent regulation and housing construction for both developed countries and developing countries since the 1980s [43, 44].

Against such evidence, one ought to treat with caution any interest groups and lawmakers who are calling for rent caps, especially which include laws restricting rent growth across tenancies as well as lease period legislation.

## 5.2. The effects of rent controls on housing markets

In this section, we examine the theoretical arguments, including merits and demerits of their use in public policy, that underpin rent controls as instruments of government engagement in the residential rental sector. An early formulation of bid rent and housing choice was produced in the classic work of Alonso [2]. Fujita [28] later proposed a coherent framework for using the bid rent model in urban land use and city structure studies. In this framework, household location and housing choice influence bid rents.

From this, a rent gradient rule may be developed. Small households are more likely to be located in the centre of an urban region, whilst large households are more likely to be found in areas remote from the centre of the urban region. Assume that a household's utility is defined as a function of the consumption of a composite good c and the size of the dwelling unit b. The consumer's choice problem is thus:

$$\max U = u(c,\ b)$$
$$\text{subject to:}\ y = c + P\ (d)b + R(d) \qquad (5.1)$$

where $U$ represents a utility function that is at least twice differentiable and concave. If $y$ denotes household income, $P$ denotes the price of housing based on the size b at location $d$, and $R$ denotes the rent per square metre based on the distance d between a place and the urban city centre. This problem's Lagrangian is:

$$\max_{c,b,d,\lambda} L = u(c,\ b) - \lambda(c + P\ (d)b + R(d)\ y) \qquad (5.2)$$

and the maximisation conditions are:

$$\frac{\delta L}{\delta c} = \frac{\delta u}{\delta c} - \lambda = 0$$
$$\frac{\delta L}{\delta b} = \frac{\delta u}{\delta b} - \lambda p(d) = 0$$
$$\frac{\delta L}{\delta d} = -\lambda \left[ \frac{\delta P}{\delta d} b - \frac{\delta R}{\delta d} \right] = 0 \qquad (5.3)$$
$$\frac{\delta L}{\delta \lambda} = c + P(d)b + R(d) - y = 0$$

If $\lambda \neq 0$ then

$$\frac{\delta P}{\delta d} = -\frac{\delta R}{\delta u}\frac{1}{b} \qquad (5.4)$$

Consider a monocentric city with a Central Business District (CBD). If the marginal change in housing price with regard to distance from the metropolitan centre equals the marginal change in rent with respect to distance divided by housing quantity, the household's decision set is optimal.

Assuming equal household income levels, this means that small households (demanding minimal b) will seek to move closer to the metropolitan centre than bigger families (demanding a bigger amount of housing). Figure 3 depicts the bid-rent curves for the two kinds of family units, where bs < bl.

According to the model, tiny families in the usual situation will be located in the core areas of an urban area, but big households at a given income level will be located farther out from the metropolitan centre. In Figure 3, the position (distance from CBD) that acts as a dividing point in the urban zone is shown by the intersection of the two rent gradients (bidrent curves). If d < d0, bs dominates; if d > d0, bl dominates. In actuality, a significant number of bid-rent curves overlap each other practically continually across long distances. The top envelope of these bidrent functions would be found in the housing rent structure of a metropolitan uncontrolled market.

A rent restriction, according to a conventional comparative-static model of the housing sector, lowers owner incomes, raises house costs, and suppresses investment rewards. Housing stock depreciates with time. This result tends to make the analysis less than straightforward for second-generation rent controls, according to some scholars [4, 56, 45]. Setting the market into a controlled and a free segment (for example, dwellings constructed before/after a certain date) will have a beneficial impact on free-market rentals, providing an opportunity to invest. This section specifies that misallocation causes this beneficial impact on free-market rentals, and therefore can be seen as the foundation for an empirical examination of misallocation.

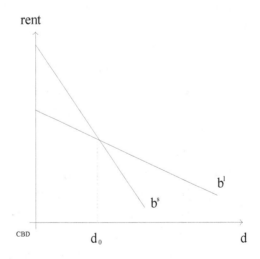

Figure 3: The rent gradient for households

Figure 4: Misallocation under 1st and 2nd generation rent controls

a.  First-generation rent control                    b.  Second-generation rent control

Source: Mense et al. (2018)[53]

Since housing is both immobile and resilient, separate regional market equilibria occur. Furthermore, property markets are segmented both spatially and qualitatively. Households can substitute rental payments for commuting costs and move to the periphery of the market as demand and therefore rents in city centres increase. On the one side, business interconnectedness is ideal for identifying counterfactuals for consumer trends in both controlled and unregulated regions. The free sectors of the industry, on the other side, are often impacted by the control of a particular sub-segment.

Figure 4 depicts this influence using a traditional comparative-static paradigm. First, consider an uncontrolled economy where housing demand ($D$) falls as the rent rises (vertical axis). The market is in equilibrium as it intersects with the perfectly inelastic short-run housing supply ($S_s$), delivering hs units of housing services (a function of housing quantity and quality). In an ideal world, the short-run equilibrium is the same as the long-run demand-supply balance $(S_l)$. The costs of new construction, repair, and refurbishment decide the slope of the long-run supply curve. As long as residential demand covers building utility development prices, the housing supply grows. Rents are limited to a degree below market equilibrium, which reduces refurbishment effort and allows depreciation to outpace new housing production. We abstract from certain supply consequences, at least for now.

Consider the implementation of a rent management system. The controlled price in first generation rent regulation extends to the whole industry. When the marginal costs of renting out a unit outweigh the controlled price, supply falls to $S_c$, meaning a lack of (rental) housing units of $h_s$-$h_c$. Households who may have been compelled to flee the sector if rent regulation did not exist will still bid for apartments in the area. Households are assigned to dwellings by methods rather than ability to pay, such as lottery, queuing, or nepotism. The welfare deficit due to misallocation under random distribution is equivalent to the red tetragon.

The controlled price in second-generation rent regulation only extends to a portion of the economy (right side of Figure 4). The housing stock hs is divided into two segments: a limited segment $(h_c)$ and a free-market segment $(h_s h_c)$. Housing units are distributed by ability to pay in the free-market segment. Assume that the regulated segment's distribution is random. This means that rent-managed households are a random subset of all households whose ability to pay exceeds the controlled price.

Thus, $D_f$ connects the intersection of $S_c$ and the maximum ability to pay $r_{max}$ with the intersection of the controlled price and $D_f$ in the free-market part. The implementation of a rent limit in this situation raises the price of new homes from the original to the new free market price. The arbitrary assignment of households to rent managed units is the guiding force behind this outcome. Another reason for higher unregulated unit prices may be a decrease in availability of managed units due to transfer to owner-occupied status. Then, even though there is no misallocation, a positive spillover to free market rentals may be observed: The decreased supply would cause the demand curve to shift upwards. Unless a significant portion of the rental housing stock is converted, which we believe is very doubtful in the near term, this sort of spillover is arguably quite limited.

The red tetragon represents wellbeing loss due to mis-allocation. The related portion of the demand curve is located between the two vertical dotted red lines; these households have a propensity to pay that is lower than the free-market price but higher than the controlled price. Since these families are assigned to rent-controlled units at random, the average market valuation in this category is what counts for welfare (depicted by the horizontal dashed red line).

The straightforward graphical representation has a number of intriguing implications. Rent regulation causes a rise in free-market prices when it lowers rents in the regulated industry. Prices of building lots where modern, uncontrolled homes can be built may also rise, since home prices are dictated by potential rental revenue. Finally, favourable results on new development can be expected if land availability is elastic. Negative effects on housing stock and community sorting are also possible, according to previous research. These latter results, on the other hand, are expected to take longer to manifest.

Rent stabilisation measures have been justified in the expert literature because of the potential improvements in social well-being resulting from the assurances that these policies give to residents. The benefits will be particularly important where residential rental rates are less stable and policies favour low-income renters. Various scholars, on the other hand, argue that residential rent controls can cause inefficiencies in the housing sector, with potentially negative consequences for social well-being [35].

In terms of the potential costs of rent controls, although these measures increase the social well-being of the tenants who are impacted immediately, the shift of incentives triggered by the legislation triggers reactions on both the supply and demand sides that which result in a loss of social well-being in the medium and long term. According to economic theory, if managed residential rentals are set at a below-market rate, the stock of rental housing would decrease. This is due to a greater opportunity for tenants to sell their homes, as well as a decrease in spending in the development or rehabilitation of rental properties. Around the same period, the resulting decrease in total gain on investment in residential accommodation will result in lower building upkeep and construction costs, lowering the property's efficiency over time.

Furthermore, if the legislation resulted in a dual residential rental market, where rent-controlled assets coexisted with free-market rentals in separate parts of the same region, there might be additional productivity losses. Tenants can have an opportunity to stay in properties with controlled rentals that are below market price in segmented rental markets. Which reduces workplace mobility and induces detrimental externalities by disproportionately concentrating the workforce in some parts of the city and causing a housing stock misallocation. In particular, if they were to relocate, the potential lack of controlled housing would cause households that are expanding (shrinking) in size to stay in limited (large) housing units, resulting in inefficiencies in the rental housing stock distribution. Furthermore, in a rent-controlled market, the decrease in rental return on investment and population segmentation may reduce the aggregate value of real estate assets. Finally, a decrease in the total availability of residential rentals tends to boost rental rates in non-regulated market segments. This impact may be very strong in situations where demand is increasing and rental housing is in short supply.

We should mention that there are theoretical arguments to the effect that laws that limit rent growth can be advantageous to social well-being [4, 25]. These points are founded on the non-competitive existence of the rental industry in situations where landlords can establish rental rates, looking for rental housing is expensive, and there are no price guarantee systems in place for renters. In particular, social well-being benefits would occur where rent-hike laws provide renters with a promise, as opposed to an asymmetrical business arrangement in which tenants would pay to move and the owner has market control. Similarly, an automated rent upgrade process over a set time eliminates resident volatility in terms of job and consumption decisions. Furthermore, rent control laws are justified in the face of beneficial externalities correlated with the accumulation of social (community) resources by households in their communities. For example, the prospect of a sharp, unanticipated increase in rents would deter households from engaging in a neighbourhood in case they had to relocate, and if they did relocate, the social capital they had built up would be lost.

Favilukis et al. (2019) [25] investigate the changes in social well-being resulting from pledge processes in the context of a spatial model that quantitatively assesses the impact of policies that include sub-market rental accommodation. They often pinpoint the contexts in which certain policies produce those results. When rent limits are focused on families at the lower end of the income spectrum, redistribution policies in the context of rent controls will produce improvements in social well-being in the face of price rises, amid potential rental market distortions. Rent caps are a safety net in an environment where rents can rise at an unpredictable rate over time, such as in urban areas where household income disparity and polarisation are strong.

In this scenario, these benefits might be sufficient to compensate for social well-being losses caused by spatial misallocation of housing among households or inefficient sectoral job position as a consequence of price controls.

Autor et al. [7, 8] examined the impact of price restrictions in US metropolitan regions, finding productivity losses from price management and social well-being benefits from the resulting removal of rent controls. This evidence demonstrates how rent controls lowered the valuation of not just rented housing but also the properties and amenities in the neighbourhoods where rent-controlled housing was concentrated. Furthermore, after rent caps were lifted, private construction soared in deregulated neighbourhoods, leading to a decline in crime rates.

Paul Samuelson, the second Nobel Laureate in Economics was one of the most vocal opponents. In a 1999 interview, Samuelson cited rent controls as a prime example of bad legislation:

> *When one considers problems like rent control, where you'd like to sponsor Robin Hood in favor of the poor, you realize that the whole country of*

*France had no residential building between World War I and World War II, primarily for the reason of permanent rent controls. That did not achieve the good life for the poor at the expense of the rich. Rent control created deadweight loss.[3]*

Rent controls come in a variety of shapes and sizes. Controls that are relatively rigid, such as those in place in France during the interwar period, are referred to as 'first generation' controls. Some people, especially tenants who have already moved in, can profit from these controls. Rent caps had the effect of transferring capital from owners to renters, as well as improving tenants' state of mind. Rate cap opponents are not oblivious to these possible gains, but they usually argue that the risks of rent caps outweigh the advantages. This viewpoint is reflected in Samuelson's argument that rent controls result in 'deadweight loss.' This deadweight loss is graphically depicted in Figure 4, which depicts the classical economic interpretation of the consequences of rent controls. Rent regulation opponents often argue that there are more effective and tailored approaches to assist eligible residents.

They are universally viewed as an ineffective measure for supporting the long-term supply of decent housing at reasonable prices. Moreover, it is well-supported by the

[3] Samuelson on Economics and Behaviour, Dec. 25, 2009, available at http://www.pbs.org/newshour/making-sense/samuelson-on-economics-and-beh

evidence that even second-generation rent caps frequently have unintended consequences. According to Arnott [5]:

There has been widespread agreement that rent controls discourage new construction, cause abandonment, retard maintenance, reduce mobility, generate mismatch between housing units and tenants, exacerbate discrimination in rental housing, create black markets, encourage the conversion of rental to owneroccupied housing, and generally short-circuit the market mechanism for housing.

Observational studies of the influence of the regulations on rental price levels tend to agree with theoretical predictions of the regulations' harmful impacts. Most of the available studies concentrate on the experiences of a variety of big US cities and show that rent caps have negative consequences. Diamond et al.'s 2019 study [16], is one such example. The authors show how rent control regulations in San Francisco reduced the availability of cheap housing and affected the composition of that housing, resulting in increased rental rates, gentrification, and wider income gaps at the local level. In the near term, rate limitations were effective in limiting housing migrations among lower-income households, particularly among racial minorities, reducing mobility among individuals in rent-controlled districts. In the medium to long term, however, landlords' reactions resulted in a drop in the supply of rental accommodation for low-income households. As a result of these rules, there has been a surge in the construction of dwellings for higher-income households, housing upgrades (to skirt the reach of the regulations), and housing sales. Overall, the program appears to have added to demographic segmentation and reduced affordable housing availability, contributing to the city's growing rental rates.

## 6. Conclusion

In a well-functioning market, economic choices and prices of products and services are completely determined by the interactions between individuals and businesses. These conditions must exist for the market and its participants to function freely. People and businesses in a marketplace are governed by institutions that form and regulate the coordination of their economic conduct. The goal of promoting economic freedom may be ascribed to the institutions that define the free market economy. Individuals have the freedom to use, exchange, and give away their property as long as they do not infringe on the rights of others to their own property. Economic freedom is characterized by low taxation, the preservation of individual property rights, the lack of trade barriers, and minimum government intervention in finance, labor, and product markets. The role of government in a free market system is confined to ensuring that property rights and acquisition methods are legally protected.

The policy reality in California is increasingly becoming divorced from these principles. Various state laws and regulations affect house construction in California, some of which promote it and others which deliberately hinder it. A recent Brookings Institute analysis shows that when compared to other states, California's policy regime is an outlier: the state's housing market interventions are unmatched in their scale and scope. We therefore posit that the solution to the current crisis is not more government, but less – at least in the sense that there ought to be less intervention/distortion of the housing markets.

Policymakers should to aim towards housing outcomes, such as increased housing production and greater affordability, rather than focus on narrowly interpreted 'rules-based' approaches. As an illustration, current zoning reform initiatives at the state and local level lean toward pre-emption of certain activities. Initiatives to legalize duplexes have been framed as "ending single-family zoning" [46].

Because of overlapping regulations (building codes, historic preservation, zoning, environmental rules), housing production is impacted by a wide range of specialized rules. To prevent undesirable growth, local governments and communities might utilize a variety of tactics, including apartment bans, huge minimum lot sizes, and discretionary approval processes. Whilst focusing on the bigger picture, such as increasing housing supply and decreasing housing costs, policymakers should try to avoid creating unnecessary political squabbles. As a result of this, state policy interventions are more likely to work if they are clearly defined and linked to sensible metrics. Similarly, when it comes to housing subsidies for low-income families, it is important to look at how many people are assisted rather than how much money is spent. As a result of this, state policy interventions are more likely to work if they are clearly defined and linked to sensible metrics.

A barometer of a well-functioning housing markets is when developers build more homes in areas where people wish to live (e.g. locations with strong demand). Housing markets must provide a wide range of options for workers with varying wages in order for businesses to recruit and retain employees (e.g., by home size, tenure, and price range). Because of existing transportation infrastructure, regional labor markets are dependent on workers' ability to live within a commutable distance of their workplaces.

The cost of housing in California is significantly higher than the national average, which exacerbates homelessness and poverty while also compressing household budgets to the extent that they significantly reduce the standard of living, particularly for middle and low-income families in the state. As a result of rules and regulations that raise the cost of building and/or limit development, housing prices and rents have increased considerably in the Bay Area, Silicon Valley, Los Angeles, and Orange County as well as San Diego. As we have argued in this chapter, the housing problem in California is mostly the result of shortages in the state's housing supply.

Housing development choices are determined at the municipal level, but the need for additional housing is felt statewide. Transferring certain land-use authority from local governments to state governments has some practical and political obstacles. Most state governments have not dealt directly with land use or housing supply in the past, hence staff capability would need to be built up. The relationship between state legislatures and municipal governments can be tense, particularly between Republican-controlled legislatures and Democratic mayors of major cities. Housing issues are not neatly correlated with traditional partisan differences; increasing state participation has the potential to enhance housing results, but it is not without risk.

Policymakers in California should, therefore, enact reforms to address policy congestion reforms such as limiting the impact of urban growth boundaries as well as other landuse restrictions in order to allow for more housing construction, removing regulations that arbitrarily raise construction costs such as prevailing wage requirements, and restricting the fees charged for building permits.

Significant legislative reforms are required if the state is to increase housing supply and lower costs. To make a significant difference, a broad variety of policy changes are required. There has been an increase in the cost of construction in California because of bureaucratic hurdles put in place by the state's regulators. Also included in the list of suggestions are changes to CEQA, which is being misused in entirely unexpected ways to prevent or delay building and collect fines from developers for special-interest groups.

Sensible and coordinated political thinking is needed at both the state and municipal levels to break the decades-long grip the status quo has had on growth and to generate an affordability crisis that severely impacts the state's most economically disadvantaged inhabitants. In order to improve the quality of life for all Californians, voters must put pressure on their elected leaders to make intelligent policy choices to ensure the state's economic vitality.

The answer to California's housing affordability dilemma is to build a regulatory framework that strikes a balance between economic growth, housing affordability, and development sustainability while also protecting the environment. At the same time, it is critical to safeguard California's unique historical legacy, as well as devise a growth strategy that handles transportation congestion and growing public utilities. More housing, particularly multifamily housing units, is required, and this may be accomplished while taking into account the other factors. According to a 2018 study by Herkenhoff et al, restoring California's land-use laws to 2000 levels would double the state's population and produce an additional $800 billion in income and productivity.

# Bibliography

[1] Alpanda S., Zubairy, S. 2016 'Housing and Tax Policy', Journal of Money Credit and Banking Vol.48/2-3 pp. 485-512

[2] Alonso W. (1964) Location and Land Use. Harvard University Press. Cambridge Mass.

[3] Andersen H.S. (1998) 'Motives for investments in housing rehabilitation among private landlords under rent control' Housing Studies 13 (2) 177–200.

[4] Arnott R., Igarashi, M., (2000). 'Rent control mismatch costs and search efficiency'. Regional Science and Urban Economics 30 (3) 249–288.

[5] Arnott R. (1995). 'Time for revisionism on rent control'. Journal of Economic Perspectives 9 (1) 99–120. [6] Ault R., Saba R., (1990). 'The economic effects of long-term rent control: The case of New York City', The Journal of Real Estate Finance and Economics 3 (1) 25–41.

[7] Autor D.H., Palmer C.J., Pathak P.A., (2014) 'Housing market spillovers: Evidence from the end of rent control in Cambridge Massachusetts', Journal of Political Economy 122 (3) 661–717.

[8] Autor D.H., Palmer C.J., Pathak P.A., (2019) 'Ending Rent Control Reduced Crime in Cambridge', AEA Papers and Proceedings, 109: 381-84.

[9] Betin M., Ziemann V., 2019 'How responsive are housing markets in the OECD? Regional level estimates', OECD Economics Department Working Papers No. 1590 OECD Publishing Paris https://dx.doi.org/10.1787/1342258c-en

[10] Brown Calder, V.. 2017. "Zoning, Land-Use Planning, and Housing Affordability." Cato Institute Policy Analysis no. 823 (October).

[11] Cavalleri M., Cournrde B.,Ozsogut E., 2019 'How Responsive Are Housing Markets in the OECD? National Level Estimates', OECD Economics Department Working Papers No. 1589 OECD Publishing Paris.

[12] CEQA: California Environmental Quality Act Statute and Guidelines, "15195. Residential Infill Exemption," 2019 (Palm Desert, CA: Association of Environmental Professionals, 2019), pp. 243–44.

[13] Cournede B., Sakha S., Ziemann V., (2019) 'Empirical links between housing markets and economic resilience', No 1562 OECD Economics Department Working Papers, OECD Publishing.

[14] Crump, S., Schuetz, J., Mattos, T. and Schuster, L., 2020. Zoned Out: Why Massachusetts Needs to Legalize Apartments Near Transit.

[15] Dain, A. 2019. The state of zoning for multifamily housing in Greater Boston. Report for Massachusetts Housing Partnership. https://www.housingtoolbox.org/writable/files/resources/AMY-DAIN_MultiFamily_Housing_Report.pdf

[16] Diamond R., McQuade T., and Qian F., 2019 'The effects of rent control expansion on tenants landlords and inequality: Evidence from san francisco', American Economic Review Vol. 109/9 pp. 3365-3394 [17] Dillon, L. 2017. "A Key

Reform of California's Environmental Law Hasn't Kept Its Promises," Los Angeles Times, January 24, 2017, www.latimes.com/politics/ la-pol-sacenvironmental-law-reform-failures-20170124-story.html

[18] Dougherty, C. 2020. Golden Gates: Fighting for Housing in America. New York: Penguin Press.

[19] Early D., Phelps J., (1999). 'Rent regulations' pricing effect in the uncontrolled sector: An empirical investigation', Journal of Housing Research 10 (2) 267–285.

[20] Early D. W., (2000) 'Rent control rental housing supply and the distribution of tenant benefits', Journal of Urban Economics 48 (2) 185–204.

[21] Einstein, K.L., Palmer, M. and Glick, D.M., 2019. Who participates in local government? Evidence from meeting minutes. Perspectives on politics, 17(1), pp.28-46.

[22] Elmendorf, C.S., Biber, E., Monkkonen, P. and O'Neill, M., 2021. "I Would, If Only I Could" How Cities Can Use California's Housing Element Law to Overcome Neighborhood Resistance to New Housing. How Cities Can Use California's Housing Element Law to Overcome Neighborhood Resistance to New Housing. Willamette Law Review.

[23] Elmendorf, C.S., Biber, E., Monkkonen, P. and O'Neill, M., 2021. State Administrative Review of Local Constraints on Housing Development: Improving the California Model. Arizona Law Review, Forthcoming.

[24] Fallis G., Smith L. B. (1984) 'Uncontrolled prices in a controlled market: The case of rent controls', The American Economic Review 74 (1) 193–200.

[25] Favilukis, J., Mabille P., Van Nieuwerburgh S., (2019) 'Affordable housing and city welfare', NBER Working Paper No. 25906.

[26] Fischel W. 2001 'The Homevoter Hypothesis: How Home Values Influence Local Government Taxation, School, Finance, and Land-Use Policies', Harvard University Press.

[27] Fisher, L.M. and Marantz, N.J., 2015. Can state law combat exclusionary zoning? Evidence from Massachusetts. Urban Studies, 52(6), pp.1071-1089.

[28] Fujita M., (1989) 'Urban Economic Theory, Land Use and City Size', Cambridge University Press, Cambridge

[29] Furman Center for Real Estate and Urban Policy (2011). Rent Stabilization in New York City

[30] Furth, S. and Gonzalez, O., 2019. California Zoning: Housing Construction and a New Ranking of Local Land Use Regulation. Mercatus Research Paper.

[31] Garde, A. and Song, Q., 2021. Housing Affordability Crisis and Inequities of Land Use Change: Insights From Cities in the Southern California Region. Journal of the American Planning Association, pp.1-16. [32] Ganong, P. and Shoag, D., 2017. Why has regional income convergence in the US declined?. Journal of Urban Economics, 102, pp.76-90.

[33] Glaeser, E.L., Gyourko, J. and Saks, R.E., 2005. Why have housing prices gone up?. American Economic Review, 95(2), pp.329-333.

[34] Glaeser E. L. (2003). Does rent control reduce segregation? Swedish Economic Policy Review 10 179–202.

[35] Glaeser, E.L. and Kahn, M.E., 2010. The greenness of cities: Carbon dioxide emissions and urban development. Journal of urban economics, 67(3), pp.404-418.

[36] Gray, M.N. and Furth, S., 2019. Do minimum-lot-size regulations limit housing supply in Texas?. Mercatus Research Paper.

[37] Gyourko J., Molloy R., 2015 'Regulation and Housing Supply', Handbook of Regional and Urban Economics Vol. 5 pp. 1289-1337

[38] Gyourko J., Saiz A., Summers A., 2008 'A New Measure of the Local Regulatory Environment for Housing Markets: The Wharton Residential Land Use Regulatory Index' Urban Studies Vol. 45/3 pp. 693-729.

[39] Herkenhoff, K.F., Ohanian, L.E. and Prescott, E.C., 2018. Tarnishing the golden and empire states: Land-use restrictions and the US economic slowdown. Journal of Monetary Economics, 93, pp.89-109.

[40] Hernandez, J., Friedman, D. and DeHerrera, S., 2015. In the Name of the Environment: How Litigation Abuse Under the California Environmental Quality Act Undermines California's Environmental, Social Equity and Economic Priorities–and Proposed Reforms to Protect the Environment from CEQA Litigation Abuse. Holland and Knight LLP.

[41] Hsieh, C.T. and Moretti, E., 2019. Housing constraints and spatial misallocation. American Economic Journal: Macroeconomics, 11(2), pp.1-39.

[42] Jones, C. and Kammen, D.M., 2014. Spatial distribution of US household carbon footprints reveals suburbanization undermines greenhouse gas benefits of urban population density. Environmental science and technology, 48(2), pp.895-902.

[43] Kholodilin K. A. Kohl S. (2020). Does social policy through rent controls inhibit new construction? Some answers from long-run historical evidence (DIW Berlin Discussion Paper 1839). Berlin: DIW Berlin.

[44] Kholodilin K. A. (2020). Long-term multicountry perspective on rental market regulations. Housing Policy Debate 30 (6) 994–1015.

[45] Kutty N. K. (1996). The impact of rent control on housing maintenance: A dynamic analysis incorporating European and North American rent regulations. Housing Studies 11 (1) 69–88.

[46] Los Angeles Times Editorial Board. 2021. Editorial: Watch out, NIMBYs. Newsom just dumped single family zoning. https://www.latimes.com/opinion/story/2021-09-17/newsom-housing-sb9

[47] Linneman P. (1987). The effect of rent control on the distribution of income among New York City renters. Journal of Urban Economics 22 (1) 14–34.

[48] Manville, M. and Monkkonen, P., 2021. Unwanted Housing: Localism and Politics of Housing Development. Journal of Planning Education and Research, p.0739456X21997903.

[49] Marks D. (1984). The effect of rent control on the price of rental housing: an hedonic approach. Land Economics 60 (1) 81–94.

[50] Mawhorter, S. and Reid, C. (2018). "Terner California Residential Land Use Survey." Terner Center for Housing Innovation, UC Berkeley.

[51] McFarlane A. (2003). Rent stabilization and the long-run supply of housing. Regional Science and Urban Economics 33 (3) 305–333.

[52] Mense A. Michelsen C. and Kholodilin K. A. (2017). Empirics on the causal effects of rent control in Germany. FAU Discussion Papers in Economics 24/2017.

[53] Mense A. C. Michelsen and K. Kholodilin (2019). Rent Control Market Segmentation and Misallocation: Causal Evidence from a Large-Scale Policy Intervention. Discussion paper no. 1832 DIW Berlin.

[54] Moon C.-G. and J. G. Stotsky (1993). The effect of rent control on housing quality change: A longitudinal analysis. Journal of Political Economy 1114–1148.

[55] Ohanian, L.E., 2021. Common-Sense Policy Reforms for California Housing. Cato Institute, Policy Analysis, (920).

[56] Olsen E. (1988a). Economics of rent control. Journal of Real Estate Finance and Economics 28 673–678. [57] Rothwell, J., 2019. Land Use Politics, Housing Costs, and Segregation in California Cities. Berkeley, CA: University of California, Berkley, Terner Center for Housing Innovation.

[58] Sommer K. and P. Sullivan 2018 'Implications of US Tax Policy for House Prices Rents and Homeownership' American Economic Review Vol. 108/2 pp. 241-274

[59] Schuetz, Jenny. 2022. Fixer Upper: How to repair America's Broken Housing Systems. Washington DC: Brookings Institution Press. (forthcoming)

[60] Thompson, E. Jr., 2009. "Agricultural Land Loss and Conservation," California Department of Food and Agriculture, https://www.cdfa.ca.gov/agvision/docs/Agricultural_Loss_and_Conservation.pdf

[61] Thomschke L. and S. Hein (2015). So schnell schiessen die Preußen nicht: Effekte der Mietpreisbremse in Berlin. empirica paper Nr. 226.

[62] Turner B. and S. Malpezzi (2003). A review of empirical evidence on the costs and benefits of rent control. Swedish Economic Policy Review 10 11–56.

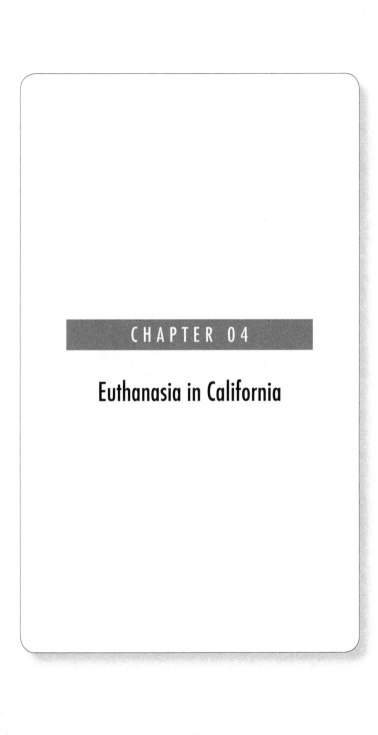

# CHAPTER 04

# Euthanasia in California

# Euthanasia in California

*Abstract*

The discussion on legalizing euthanasia and assisted suicide has a long history in the United States. The implications of legalizing euthanasia affect a broad range of parties, including physicians, scholars, politicians, lawyers, and the general public. This chapter analyzes euthanasia's ethical and philosophical perspectives and provides essential information and relevant and helpful suggestions based on up-to-date facts and foundational principles in ethical decision-making concerning end-of-life medical care in California. This chapter explores the discussion's roots and current implications, as euthanasia is currently legal in California. It also offers a comprehensive perspective of this issue from historical, ontological, ethical, sociological, religious, and cultural viewpoints because ideas and standpoints directly influence public policy and legislation. Revisiting old and ongoing debates on euthanasia and identifying common threads can engender a more enlightened perspective about current concerns with euthanasia, especially during a time when legislators are approving euthanasia worldwide. The author reviews the standard arguments supporting and opposing euthanasia throughout history, remarks on recent legal developments, particularly in the United States, and carefully analyzes the California End of Life Option Act. While legislators have made significant advancements in making the act easier to use, some potential users may still face challenges due to their advanced age and health condition.

## 1. Chapter Summary

While the Romans and the Greeks are known to have practiced euthanasia regularly, the Assyrian physicians forbade the practice in Mesopotamia. The debate on euthanasia and assisted suicide has a long history in the United States, particularly in states like Oregon and California. Legislators have attempted to introduce euthanasia-related bills based on medical and philosophical arguments several times throughout history. As public opinion on the topic was polarized, observers within the bioethics community were unsure about the 1992 California Death with Dignity Act initiative's prospects for passage into law. While the 2016 California End of Life Option Act offers a range of options for some, its requirements may limit some California residents from using it. California legislators seem to be aware that it is time to remove unnecessary barriers to access aid in dying so that all eligible terminally ill individuals can die with dignity.

## 2. Introduction to Euthanasia in California

Recently, much has been proclaimed, discussed, and analyzed on the right to die with dignity. The issue has made its way from the hospital room to the courts and parliaments. Discussions of the right to die are often confusing. Technical complexities such as the definition of brain death intertwine with careful philosophical explorations of rights and euthanasia and with cries of moral outrage expressed in condemnations of assisted suicide. The definitions of euthanasia and assisted suicide are also intertwined and very close to each other but may have different legal implications that vary from country to country.

With increasing life expectancy, cases of chronic and disabling diseases also increase. Additionally, a stronger emphasis on humanized medicine and palliative care have prompted discussions on the quality of death in many countries. Assisted death is a current and controversial topic in this scenario. The projected growth of the elderly population in developed and developing countries is also likely to lead to an increase in the number of chronic and disabling diseases.

At the heart of this tangled and complex debate is the question of whether a dying person should be kept alive by medical treatment. Behind this question is the sometimes tacit but often loud accusation that doctors keep dying people alive for nothing—or worse, for their own purposes and vain interests. Doctors are accused of being insensitive to the dying, not understanding death, and not letting go. Unlike their predecessors, who honestly acknowledged the arrival of death's blessed relief, modern doctors are said to push death away from the bedside with a bevy of breathing, beating machines.

Over time, especially following the Scientific Revolution and introduction of analgesics (cocaine) and anesthetics (ether), medical conceptions have progressed from pain being seen as a punishment for sins to an external element that enters the body and finally to a series of independent, internal pathways (a theory Descartes proposed). The reduction of pain, particularly at the end of life, has been historically recognized as a legitimate goal of medicine. Understanding this fact is crucial for a better understanding of modern-day assisted suicide and euthanasia stances. The issue remains open to philosophical, political, and legal challenges (Fernandes, 2001, pp. 124, 127).

In the United States, the topic of euthanasia has been debated repeatedly since the nineteenth century. However, public support for euthanasia has never been higher. As the Supreme Court has not directly ruled on whether legislation permitting a doctor or physician to prescribe life-ending treatment is constitutional, states, such as Oregon, Vermont, and California, have taken to legislating the issue themselves.

Amanda Thyden points out that California passed its own End of Life Option Act, following the acceptance of the right-to-die movement in Oregon, Vermont, Washington, and Montana. This act mirrors those of the other states and requires Californians to ask for life-ending medication verbally or in writing two times, at least 15 days apart[4], to ensure that they have the chance to reflect on the decision to end their lives. It also requires a physician to refer a patient to a physician counselor if they believe that the patient may require a psychological evaluation. Finally, it requires that a patient have the capacity to self-administer the medication. This last requirement puts the final act of medication consumption in the hands of the patient (Thyden, 2017, p. 430).

Legislators' purpose in passing the California End of Life Option Act was to prevent state residents from suffering miserable deaths. The objective was to provide Californians with an option at the end of their lives: they now may choose to die naturally or in their own time. If a patient is required to administer their own life-ending drugs, then another person should not be blamed for the patient's resulting death. However, the California legislature has not clarified the exact parameters of self-administration (Thyden, 2017, p. 431).

---

[4] From January 1, 2022, this period has been changed to 48 hours.

## 2. Definitions Associated With Euthanasia and Assisted Suicide

Etymologically, the word euthanasia means good death, or in other words, death without pain, without suffering. In the twentieth century, the word took on a negative connotation when it was misused in Nazi policies to eliminate lives that society considered unworthy of existence. Currently, the practice of euthanasia is allowed in some countries. A more contemporary definition understands euthanasia as employing or withholding procedures to accelerate or induce the death of incurably ill patients to free them from extreme suffering.

Arguably, one can find the first reference to euthanasia in English literature in 1516. In Utopia, Thomas More wrote that they consoled the incurably ill by sitting and talking with them; the priests did not hesitate to prescribe euthanasia or persuade the sick to end their lives through starvation or drugs. Those who suffered from terminal diseases had the choice to die without any sensation of death if they had previously agreed on it. Later, in the 17th century, Francis Bacon stressed that science should help relieve a person's physical health arguing that the physician's duty was to restore good health and mitigate pain and discomfort (Emanuel, 1994, pp. 793–794).

Regarding the patient's consent, euthanasia can be classified as non-voluntary and voluntary—the first takes place without knowing the patient's will and the second in response to their expressed wishes. Euthanasia differs from assisted suicide because it is performed by a physician, while the patient performs the final act in assisted suicide. There is a significant difference between "killing" and "letting die" from medical and legal viewpoints. Experts divide euthanasia into active and passive. Active euthanasia denotes the deliberate act of inducing death without the patient suffering (employing, for example, poisonous injection). Passive euthanasia refers to death through the intentional omission of medical action that would prolong survival (Reis de Castro et al., 2016, p. 356).

Assisted suicide, also known as euthanasia, comprises several acts that intentionally help an individual end their life. These acts include voluntarily stopping eating and drinking, terminal sedation, physician-assisted suicide, and euthanasia, all of which are last-resort treatments in standard palliative care. The World Health Organization (WHO) (n.d.) defines palliative care as an approach that enhances quality of life for patients and their families facing the stress associated with life-threatening illnesses. Palliative care can improve quality of life through early identification, assessment, and treatment of pain and other problems, including physical, psychosocial, and spiritual.

The prevention and relief of patient suffering are not always achievable because high-quality palliative care can fail for some patients. Such patients are likely to request assisted death, ultimately finding that the burden of continued life-prolonging treatment outweighs the potential benefits, especially for terminal illnesses.

On the other hand, technical complexities such as the definition of brain death intertwine with painstaking philosophical investigations and deliberations of rights and euthanasia and with cries of moral outrage voiced in condemnations of mercy killing. At the center of the very complex discussion lies the question: should a dying person be kept alive by medical treatment?

Regarding voluntarily stopping eating and drinking, a patient decides to discontinue all oral intake and is gradually allowed to die, primarily due to dehydration. Many patients naturally lose their appetites and thus stop eating and drinking during the last stages of chronic debilitating diseases. As this form of assisted suicide is voluntary, it does not require the physician to participate. However, depending on the patient's medical condition, the process can take several weeks, lasting 1–4 weeks longer if the patient continues ingesting fluids. In addition, physicians and family members may find the process morally questionable, as the patient's death due to starvation and dehydration may be challenging to follow and support, especially as the patient will experience thirst and hunger. The patient will likely lose mental clarity and resolve toward the end of the process. This procedure raises questions of whether the action of voluntarily stopping eating and drinking remains voluntary.

## 3. Historical Background

Debates on the ethical permissibility of assisted suicide date back to ancient civilizations such as Mesopotamia, Greece, and Rome. Euthanasia has an ancient history and has been both opposed and defended throughout history. The Hippocratic School ultimately rejected the place of assisted suicide in medicine.

Humans have moral and religious values concerning creation and death of humans, which are influenced by their origin and status in society. Over time, the law has defended all these values because they are the core of the tradition. Thus, several countries' criminal codes and civil laws criticize euthanasia. Christianity found this philosophical and practical prohibition compatible with Revelation, which taught that human beings have inestimable value because they are created in the image and likeness of God. By the 15th century, most European physicians had rejected euthanasia, which remained valid until the 20th century when involuntary euthanasia emerged in Nazi Germany during the Holocaust.

Modern debates about legalizing euthanasia and physician-assisted suicide in Great Britain and the United States have their roots in the late 19th century. In 1870, nonphysician Samuel Williams first proposed using anesthetics and morphine to intentionally end a patient's life. Over the following 35 years, arguments about the ethics of euthanasia raged in the United States and Britain, which resulted in an Ohio bill to legalize euthanasia in 1906. This bill was eventually defeated (Emanuel, 1994, p. 793).

However, Ezekiel Emanuel stresses that ancient Greece and Rome and 20th-century Germany are of limited relevance in helping society understand contemporary euthanasia debates in the United States. First, Ancient Greece and Rome were pagan societies with slaves and cultural values that endorsed aristocratic and martial virtues; they also lacked well-developed medical professions. Second, Germany in the early 20th century considered the "Volk" more important than the individual and had no democratic tradition. Such differences between these societies and our own minimize their usefulness in illuminating contemporary interest in euthanasia (Emanuel, 1994, pp. 793–794). While still very relevant, understanding the ancient roots of modern-day debates of euthanasia in the United States requires carefully analyzing facts without isolating them from their cultural and historical context.

For the reasons outlined, debates that occurred in the United States and Britain that have shaped the American mentality and political culture toward euthanasia are worth analyzing. In his extensive research on euthanasia, Emanuel also states that writers and thinkers such as John Donne, Hume, Montesquieu, and other English and French philosophers questioned prohibitions against suicide as part of a general attack on religious authority.

Even if they did not directly talk about euthanasia, the topic was implicit because the arguments they invoked to justify suicide could also justify this practice. However, it was not until the 19th century that the world witnessed a revolution in the use of anesthesia. As physicians such as Warren and Bullar encouraged the use of narcotics and anesthetics for pain relief, Samuel Williams went further and advocated the use of medication to end patients' lives intentionally (Emanuel, 1994, pp. 794–795).

The latter third of the 19th century in the United States and Britain, known today as the Gilded Age, was marked by an individualistic conservatism. This individualistic conservatism praised laissez-faire economics, positivism, scientific method, and rationalism. On the other hand, it opposed authority, reverence for tradition, and sentimental bonds. The Gilded Age was a time of industrialization, corporate competition, and unprecedented clashes between labor unions and the corporations trying to crush them. It was also a time when free-market policies caused deep economic oscillations, and major depressions were sparked by the panic of 1873, the droughts of the 1880s, and the stock market crash of 1893. Appeals to Darwinism reinforced and sanctioned individualism, economic competition, and rationalism (Emanuel, 1994, pp. 795).

The publication of Williams' euthanasia proposal provoked much discussion in the medical profession. In April 1879, the South Carolina Medical Association heard a report from its ethics committee on active euthanasia; the association vigorously debated the issue and whether the discussion should be kept secret. Over the following few years, other medical societies followed the trend and began actively debating euthanasia. British and U.S. medical journals published editorials on the subject, often referring to Williams' original proposal. By the 1890s, the euthanasia debate had spread to lawyers and social scientists beyond the medical profession. Around 1890, New York lawyer Albert Bach frequently spoke at conferences advocating euthanasia. At the 1895 Medico-Legal Congress, he advocated euthanasia, arguing that patients had the right to end their lives. The debate soon entered the political forums, and in 1905–1906, Charles Eliot Norton, a renowned Harvard professor, gave a speech advocating euthanasia. His position inspired a wealthy woman, Anna Hill, whose mother had cancer, to advocate for the legalization of euthanasia in Ohio. Ohio Representative Hunt introduced an "An Act Concerning Administration of Drugs etc. to Mortally Injured and Diseased Persons," a bill to legalize euthanasia, which attracted considerable interest (Emanuel, 1994, pp. 795–796).

During the twentieth century, euthanasia-related legislation was periodically proposed in several countries only to be defeated until, in 1942, Switzerland decriminalized assistance in suicide[5] for cases when there were no selfish motives. Debates about the legalization of euthanasia continue in several countries and states. Many claims and counterclaims on both sides may not be consistent with an empirical understanding of the topic (Emanuel, 2017, p. 1).

In 1994, Oregon voters passed the Death with Dignity ballot initiative, the first of its kind in the United States of America. Since then, the law has allowed adults to end their life if they meet the following criteria: they must be Oregon residents who are terminally ill with a life expectancy of fewer than six months and be able to consciously express their will to die and receive medication in lethal doses, through voluntary self-administration, expressly prescribed by a doctor for this specific purpose. According to the Oregon Law, self-administration of these lethal drugs is not considered suicide but death with dignity. Nevertheless, it is worth noting that many Catholic hospitals have chosen not to adhere to this practice. Three years later, in a landmark case in 1997, the U.S. Supreme Court ruled that even though there was no constitutionally protected right to physician-assisted suicide, states were permitted to pass laws allowing it.

Since the law was established in 1997 and until 2020, 2,895 people have received prescriptions under the Death with Dignity Act; 1,905 people (66%) have died from

---

[5] There are still concerns about employing euthanasia and assisted suicide as synonyms since there are slight differences between both terms.

ingesting medications doctors prescribed. During 2020, the estimated rate of Death with Dignity Act deaths was 65.5 per 10,000 total deaths. Furthermore, 370 people received prescriptions for lethal doses of medications under the provisions of the Oregon Death with Dignity Act during 2020, which is a 25% increase over the 297 reported during 2019. Most patients died at home (92%) and were also enrolled in hospice care (95%). All patients whose health insurance status was known had some form of coverage.

Compared to the previous year, the percentage of patients with private insurance declined from 29% to 26%, while patients with Medicare or Medicaid Insurance increased from 70% to 74%. In recent years, the three most frequently reported end-of-life concerns were decreasing ability to participate in activities that made life enjoyable (94%), loss of autonomy (93%), and loss of dignity (72%) (Oregon Healthy Authority, 2021, pp. 5–6).

As populations age and medical and scientific betterments continue to transform and extend life, the issue has become increasingly controversial. In 2015, the world media widely publicized assisted death after the first case of legal euthanasia was carried out in Colombia. In the same year, assisted suicide was legalized in Canada and in the state of California, in the United States.

Euthanasia has since become one of the most controversial topics in global public opinion. Also, that year assisted suicide was legalized in Canada and California in the United States. Currently, assisted suicide is allowed in four Western European countries: the Netherlands, Belgium, Luxembourg, and Switzerland; two North American countries: Canada and the United States, in the state of Oregon, Washington, Montana, Vermont, and California; and Colombia, the only representative of South America. It is crucial to determine the prevalence and criteria adopted for euthanasia and assisted suicide in Western countries and examine the position of similar countries where this practice is not recognized. A better understanding of the subject appears critical for forming opinions and fostering future talks. The laws and criteria adopted to carry out this practice differ in each country. If the current trend continues, more countries will likely approve active euthanasia and physician-assisted suicide in the nearby future.

## 4. Public Opinion in the United States

National polls indicate overwhelming support for euthanasia-related legislation. In a 2015 Gallup poll, about 68% of Americans supported going one step further than physician-assisted suicide and supported euthanasia. Although danger may increase if euthanasia is legalized, statistics show that Americans favor patient autonomy and self-determination in ultimately deciding the course of their lives. Following Brittany Maynard's decision to utilize Oregon's Death with Dignity law, the Harris Poll found that 74% of Americans supported the right-to-die movement, while only 15% opposed physician-assisted suicide. The Institute of California Statistics found that 75.5% of Californians supported legislation promoting life-ending medication in California alone. The same poll found bipartisan support for California's End of Life Option Act, with 70% of Democrats and 55% of Republicans supporting the legislation (Thyden, 2017, pp. 440–441).

While the right-to-die and pro-euthanasia movement has strong opponents, facts suggest that they are not as strong as they used to be, especially if we compare current and historical trends in the United States. The Catholic Church remains a strong opponent of euthanasia, but the Catholic population continues to support the movement. Support for euthanasia and physician-assisted suicide is growing, and its opposition seems to be shrinking. From current figures, the explicit allowance of assisted administration will likely receive significant support in the near future.

Compared to the last decades of the nineteenth century, interest in euthanasia declined in Britain and the United States at the beginning of the twentieth century. This situation occurred because individualism and social Darwinism were in retreat and being replaced by the belief that the national government should promote the general welfare of the population; this belief was fostered and embodied in the Progressive movement in the United

States and the election of the Liberals in Britain. During this time, the medical profession consolidated its authority over medical education and practice. In Ohio, the legislature rejected a bill that proposed to legalize euthanasia, 79 to 23 (Emanuel, 1994, p. 796). These figures evidence that, at least in Ohio, support for euthanasia was still very low at that time.

However, interest in euthanasia revived during the 1930s. The idea of legalizing euthanasia was actively and vigorously debated in several public forums and in British and U.S. medical journals. Dr. C. Killick Millard, an advocate of compulsory vaccination and birth control, took advantage of the occasion of his Presidential Address to the Society of Medical Officers of Health in Britain to propose a bill for the legalization of euthanasia, based on the history of practices and attitudes toward euthanasia and suicide. Time magazine even ran an article portraying a suffering patient who wanted to undergo euthanasia. In 1936, a bill to legalize euthanasia was debated in the House of Lords in Britain. The bill was ultimately defeated 35 to 14 (Emanuel, 1994, pp. 796–797).

Following World War II, public opinion toward euthanasia worsened considerably due to the discovery of the Nazi death camps and the role German physicians played in genocide and supported euthanasia. It was not until the 1950s that Ganville Williams and Yale Kamisar revived the debate over the ethics of euthanasia in the British and U.S. legal literature. The first bill to legalize euthanasia since 1936 was introduced in the British Parliament in 1969. Generally speaking, interest in euthanasia has sparked widespread public discussion and concern within the medical profession. In the 1970s–1980s, euthanasia became both a point of public contention and a subject of more extensive academic debate in many countries. British and U.S. interest in euthanasia flourished at the two times in the previous century when the struggle over physician authority was most pronounced (Emanuel, 1994, pp. 797–801).

According to data, public support for physician-assisted suicide in the United States has not increased significantly in surveys since the mid-1970s. For example, support for assisted suicide in recent polls showed a deeply divided public, with 46% approving of related laws and 45% opposing them. In an extensive review of the available empirical literature, researchers indicate that Americans remain roughly divided on euthanasia and assisted suicide support. Roughly one-third support it without qualification, one-third oppose it without qualification, and another third of Americans support it under some conditions and oppose it under others. Thus, opinions are still very mixed (Fernandes, 2001).

While the American public's support for euthanasia and physician-assisted suicide is highest for hypothetical cases of unremitting pain, the empirical literature suggests that pain is not a strong determinant of interest in or use of euthanasia or physician-assisted suicide for the terminally ill.

Fundamentalism and church attendance may significantly predict negative attitudes toward euthanasia. The odds of opposition to euthanasia were 2.27 times greater for people who attend church at least once a week than for those who attend church less than once a week. Confidence in medical science and college education is not necessarily a predictor of negative attitudes toward euthanasia. However, age, income, and region have significant effects independent of religion and morality, even if they are weak predictors of attitudes independent of all other variables[6] (Jennings & Talley, 2003, pp. 50, 54).

The media has played a significant role in shaping public opinion toward topics like euthanasia. For instance, Scott Rae (1992) stressed that the media played a dominant role in public discussion during the 1990s. Campaign strategists faced the difficulty of communicating complex ontological and philosophical arguments in thirty-second commercial spots on television. Debates over the issue were full of passion that often obscured the real issues. Experts in bioethics were paraded in front of the cameras with their testimony. Some of the most moving commercial spots, particularly those in favor of

---

[6] Interestingly, this study found that opposition to euthanasia was greater among Blacks than among Whites.

legalizing euthanasia, took place in hospital rooms, intensive care units, and hospices.

Richard S. Myers (2002) noted that public opinion in the United States has moved in favor of assisted suicide in recent years. Public support for assisted suicide has been relatively stable in recent years and ultimately continues to increase for euthanasia. The situation would probably be vastly different if the Glucksberg and Quill decisions had come out the other way. Since California accounts for more than 12% of the population of the United States, the legalization of euthanasia and physician-assisted suicide in the state was significant. Various court decisions in other states, such as Montana, are slowly opening the door for the legalization of euthanasia.

The Supreme Court assessed one's right to commit assisted suicide in the 1997 case Washington v. Glucksberg. Amanda Thyden stressed that the plaintiff was a physician who counseled patients on suicide and challenged the constitutionality of a Washington law that banned assisted suicide. The U.S. Supreme Court held that one does not have a right to commit assisted suicide because the Court found that it was not a fundamental liberty interest. However, in a concurring opinion, Justice O'Connor stated that a patient suffering from intractable pain and already on the verge of death should have the right to die on their terms. Here, a Supreme Court Justice acknowledged that it may be appropriate for doctors to prescribe drugs that would hasten the death of one of their patients, appealing to the interests of both the physicians and the state. The Court, however, highlighted the difference between a physician actively killing someone and a physician letting someone die. In her concurrence, Justice O'Connor stated it should be up to the states to decide whether one has a right to die.

## 5. California End of Life Option Act

Before the California End of Life Option Act, euthanasia supporters had attempted to legalize euthanasia in the state several times. As public opinion on the topic was divided, observers and analysts within the bioethics community were unsure about the initiative's prospects for passage into law. In 1992, Scott Rae wrote that euthanasia was called aid in dying throughout the initiative. In the California Death with Dignity Act, aid in dying referred to a medical procedure that would end the life of the qualified patient in a painless, humane, and dignified manner, whether by a physician administering the means at the patient's choice or direction or by the patient's self-administration.

The euthanasia initiative was then criticized because it failed to provide adequate protection against abuse; it is debatable whether such protection can be achieved at all, as ensuring that euthanasia is entirely voluntary can be challenging, with considerable potential for abuse. In the Netherlands, for instance, there seemed to be strong evidence that euthanasia was practiced without the patient's explicit consent in a significant number of cases. The Remmelink Commission, chaired by the Dutch Attorney General, J. Remmelink, found that the physician deliberately hastened death without a specific request from the patient in 1,000 of the cases of active euthanasia and physician-assisted suicide. Most of the 8,750 cases of hastening death by withdrawing or withholding treatment were carried out without the explicit consent of the patient.

Since 2016, the California End of Life Option Act has allowed terminally ill patients to request medication from their physician that will end their life. Patients who choose to end their lives in this way and carefully follow the steps outlined in the law are not considered to have committed suicide. Physicians who help patients with this process are providing a new, legal form of end-of-life care and are not subject to legal liability or professionally sanctioned. This end-of-life option is voluntary for both patients and their physicians.

According to the California Department of Public Health, the two most common medication categories prescribed were a combination of a cardiotonic, opioid, and sedative at 82.3% and a sedative alone at 0.7%. During 2020, 662 individuals started the end-of-life option process, as set forth in the act, by explicitly making two verbal requests to their physicians at least 15 days apart.[7] A total of 262 physicians prescribed 677 persons aid-in-

---

[7] From January 1, 2022, this period has been changed to 48 hours.

dying drugs. Excluding COVID-19-related deaths, the rate of individuals who died from ingestion of aid-in-dying medication was 15.4 per 10,000 deaths based on 282,559 non-COVID-19 deaths of California residents in 2020 (California Department of Public Health, 2021, p. 4).

Of the 435 individuals who died under the California End of Life Option Act during 2020, 9.2% were under 60 years of age, 77.9% were 60–89 years of age, and 12.9% were 90 years of age and older. The median age was 74 years. Of the deceased, 87.4% were white and 50.8% female; 86.7% were receiving hospice and/ or palliative care, and 76.1% had at least some level of college education. Of the 435 individuals who died pursuant to the End of Life Option Act during the calendar year 2020, 70.8% were identified as having had malignant neoplasms (cancer). Neurological diseases such as amyotrophic lateral sclerosis and Parkinson's accounted for the second-largest underlying illness grouping, totaling 10.8%. The remaining significant categories of underlying illnesses were documented as respiratory diseases (non-cancer; 7.8%), cardiovascular diseases (5.1%), and other diseases (5.5%). The other diseases documented were the following: kidney disease (1.4%), cerebrovascular disease (1.1%), endocrine, nutritional and metabolic disease (1.1%), immune-mediated disease (0.2%), and other (1.6%; 5-6)

Previous statistics suggest that the average Californian resident who avails of the End of Life Option Act is White, over the age of 60, has at least some level of education, and is receiving some palliative care. Less than 10% of the individuals were younger than 60, indicating a strong correlation between age, health-deteriorating conditions, and use of the California End of Life Option Act.

To receive aid-in-dying medication, a patient must be 18 years old or older and a resident of California. The patient must also meet the following criteria: have a terminal disease that cannot be cured or reversed expected to result in death in the following six months, have the ability to make medical decisions, not have impaired judgment due to a mental disorder, and have the capacity to take the drug at the time they need and want to take it.

The California End of Life Option Act does not allow patients to request euthanasia in living wills or other documents. Authorized representatives, surrogates, and guardians cannot request euthanasia for a patient, even if they know the patient would have wanted it. If a patient desires to receive aid-in-dying medication, the patient and their physician must carefully follow the steps outlined in the law.

The following list is a summary of the California End of Life Option Act's key steps, but it is not exhaustive:

- The patient's attending physician (the one primarily responsible for the patient's illness) must determine that the patient's illness is terminal, meaning that it cannot be cured or reversed and that they will likely die in six months or less. The attending physician must also determine that the patient can make adequate medical choices.

- The patient must make two verbal requests, at least 15 days apart,8 and one in writing directly to their attending physician. The written request must be on a special form witnessed and signed by the patient, who must discuss this decision with their physician without anyone else present (except an interpreter, if needed) to ensure that the euthanasia decision is voluntary.

- The patient should make an appointment with a second physician (a consulting physician) who can confirm the diagnosis, prognosis, and the patient's ability to make medical choices. If either physician believes the patient may have a mental disorder, the patient must also see a mental health specialist to ensure that the patient's judgment is adequate.

The patient should discuss all the following with their physician:

- How the euthanasia drug will affect the patient and the fact that death may not be immediate.

---

8 From January 1, 2022, this period has been changed to 48 hours.

- Realistic alternatives to taking the medication, including comfort care, hospice care, palliative care, and pain control.

- Whether the patient wishes to withdraw the request.

- Whether the patient wants to notify next of kin, have another person present when taking the medication, or participate in a hospice program. The patient is not obligated to do any of these things.

- The physician should ensure the patient knows that they do not have to take the medication, even if they have already filled the prescription.

- If the patient still wants the medication, the doctor will write a prescription. Before taking the medication, the patient must sign a form stating that they are taking it voluntarily.

Concerning the drug's administration, taking the drug is the patient's choice. If the patient has already received the drug prescribed, they can take it whenever they want or not take it at all. The patient must take the drug themself. Other people can help prepare the drug and sit with the patient, but the patient must be the one to physically take it.

In this scenario, a physician's participation is only voluntary. In addition, entire facilities (such as clinics, hospitals, or nursing homes) can decide not to participate in aid in dying and can even prohibit employees and contractors from doing so. Nevertheless, physicians or facilities that do not engage in aid in dying must have a written policy for patients and cannot prevent someone from referring patients to a participating physician. Since the California End of Life Option Act requires the patient's attending physician to be the person that helps them with aid in dying, patients should learn about physician or facility policies when choosing who provides their care, if this is essential to them.

Regarding protections for the patient, the California End of Life Option Act states that two witnesses must be present when the patient signs the written claim form. The witnesses should sign the request form if they believe the patient is mentally capable of making decisions and is voluntarily requesting euthanasia. At least one of the witnesses should not be related to the patient or entitled to any part of the patient's estate, and at least one of the witnesses should be a person who does not work for the facility where the patient is being treated. A physician who has treated or diagnosed the patient cannot be a witness. The physician who assists a patient in dying must not be related to or entitled to inherit from the patient. It is a crime for anyone to try to force a patient to request or take euthanasia medication. Patients can change their minds and withdraw their request for the drug at any time, regardless of their mental state. An interpreter who helps a patient obtain euthanasia may not be related to the patient or entitled to the patient's inheritance. The law does not allow a patient's life to be ended by lethal injection, mercy killing, or active euthanasia since these measures are still illegal in California.

## 6. The Right to Die With Dignity

After considering that Oregon voters passed the Oregon Death with Dignity Act in 1994, which they reaffirmed by a large margin in a referendum in 1997, the concept of dignity is worth analyzing for a better understanding of the right to die with dignity.

Amanda Thyden points out that the U.S. Supreme Court and various states, such as California, have made significant strides regarding the right to die with dignity over the last twenty years. Even though the U.S. federal government remains hesitant to legalize a patient's right to die, states have taken steps to normalize the protection of a patient's right to a dignified death. The justification for such state legislation includes patient autonomy and self-determination, the prevention of undignified and painful deaths, and the advocacy efforts of residents of various states. Throughout history, states have served as laboratories of democracy to develop new and innovative laws. In serving as laboratories for law experimentation, the states enact new legislation, test it on their residents, and then, if successful, inspire other states to follow suit.

According to empirical evidence, the terminally ill perceive themselves as burdens to others at the end of life. The presence of the suffering person for others can evoke different responses, such as pity, revulsion, sympathy, empathy, or authentic compassion in the form of action. Over time, imputed dignity may become progressively tied to one's vulnerability. When vulnerability is seen as something unnatural, by serving no purpose but to alienate one from one's agency, exposure through pain and suffering is likewise seen as meaningless. Therefore, it is worth considering that 63% of persons who committed suicide in 2000 under the Oregon Death with Dignity Act did so, at least in part, because they felt they were a burden to their own families and friends (Fernandes, 2001, pp. 135–136).

As with the compassion argument to support euthanasia and physician-assisted suicide, the loss of dignity argument is not precisely formulated. Instead, it exists in a variety of expressions. Proponents of euthanasia and physician-assisted suicide argue that terminal illness, with its associated loss of control and pain and suffering, removes human dignity and that the deliberate death of the patient allows them to die with dignity. A person is a locus of meaning and value and has a center of activity. It matters, therefore, how they die as they should conduct themself according to their own standards, setting their goals and deciding how to achieve them. The patient feels alienated from themself, those they love, and the community at large. Ultimately, the perception of a loss of dignity rests on this sensation of isolation. This argument implies that dignity is important enough to allow one to kill oneself to preserve it, as allowing a hopelessly ill patient to die with dignity is one of medicine's most essential purposes.

The elements associated with the notion of dignity that one can lose due to disease are control, autonomy, integrity, identity, and choice. Terminal illness generally involves life conditions that generate severe, prolonged pain and a loss of control over bodily and mental functions. The experience or the prolongation of this suffering has negative, deleterious effects on a person's perception of their identity, integrity, independence, and autonomy. The adverse effects progressively remove a person's dignity, an essential value worth preserving. If a person chooses, they should have access to physician-assisted suicide or euthanasia. Such a free choice would preserve dignity by allowing a person to control the timing and manner of their death.

Supporters of euthanasia and physician-assisted suicide are concerned with personal and attributed dignity since basic dignity cannot be taken away from a human being; it is inherent to the human condition. Personal and attributed dignity can be removed or degraded through sickness, pain, and suffering. Human beings have intrinsic dignity due to their nature. Humans are unrepeatable beings whose value is experienced and grasped through contact with other humans. Dignity and its demands are therefore independent of culture.

Characterizing dignity as a call and a demand is especially poignant when one reminds oneself of the nature of the physician–patient relationship. The vulnerable terminally ill patient seeking medical care is demanding recognition of their intrinsic dignity; they are calling for a restoration of the toll that pain and suffering have inflicted on their imputed personal and attributed dignity. The authentic healing relationship of the healthcare giver and the suffering sick is, therefore, an opportunity to uphold the value of both physician and patient.

Opponents of euthanasia have argued that basic dignity cannot be lost and that the concept of dignity itself is vague. Fernandes stresses that dignity cannot be legitimately offered by either side in the euthanasia and physician-assisted suicide debate (although it regularly is). As a vague concept, dignity should be integrated with other, broader conceptions, especially respect for autonomy. Bioethicist Ruth Macklin has suggested that the term is useless and poorly defined, particularly in bioethics. In 1983, the President's Commission Report highlighted that the phrase "with dignity" has been used in conflicting ways since its meaning is unclear and blurred.

In California, even before the Karen Ann Quinlan case made headlines of modern-day issues regarding euthanasia and prolonging human lives, a young California legislator, Assemblyman Barry Keene, had already sensed the public concern over prolonging death. In 1974, Keene authored a bill that declared the following: "Every person has the right to die without prolongation of life by medical means." He held hearings, consultations, and debates and produced a nuanced piece of legislation known as the Natural Death Act based on this proclamation. Apart from winning the enthusiastic endorsement of many interested political parties and the cautious approval of the California Medical Association, this act also won the eventual non-opposition of the Roman Catholic hierarchy of California (Jonsen, 1978, p. 514).

For the first time in the history of the United States, the California Natural Death Act established a statutory right to die or, more appropriately, a right to be allowed to die. The existence and recognition of this right probably relieved many attending physicians' anxiety and many people's suffering. However, the existence of such a right imposed a duty on attending physicians to desist from medical care or at least a certain kind of medical care. While the patient's right to die clarified some legal obscurities, the physician's duty to desist had also created some profound ethical perplexities (Jonsen, 1978, pp. 516–517). Even if treatment is still going to occur, physicians should judge the imminence of death before initiating medical courses. Patients have the right to decide if they want to go through long, distressing, expensive, painful, and sometimes useless courses of treatment or not; they have the right to refuse.

Patients and physicians must plan early to avoid the ultimate ethical perplexities of emergency and intensive care. The emergence of an honest and ethical approach to terminal illness and medicine devoted to easing rather than preventing death may make such planning more accessible than ever before. The intervening treatment should acknowledge the imminence or proximity of death to preserve a patient's right to die with dignity (Jonsen, 1978, p. 520). This controversial act evidenced how important it is that physicians recognize the limits of their skills to reverse the course of a terminal disease since there are profound ethical implications in continuing the treatment of a very ill human being. In its broad sense, the California Natural Death Act allowed passive euthanasia in California because patients can reject medical treatment.

## 7. Limits and Requirements

Explicitly addressing the self-administration requirement, Amanda Thyden writes that the California End of Life Option Act unreasonably limits the options for Californians approaching the end of their lives. This requirement dramatically limits much-needed access to life-ending medications, but also, in practice, the self-administration requirement is unnecessary because of its expansive interpretation (Thyden, 2017, p. 421). Self-administration requires the patient to administer the medication to themself. While this requirement may silence some critics and is said to protect a patient's right to self-determination, it excludes anyone who cannot physically self-administer medication from taking advantage of the rights granted by the California End of Life Option Act. Many terminally ill patients with mobility issues may want to end their lives on their own terms and should not be excluded from this legislation (Thyden, 2017, p. 422).

Legislation should be inclusive rather than exclusive in this case. Experts are continuously proposing changes and amendments to the California End of Life Option Act further to improve the quality of life of state residents. The justification for those changes lies in preventing undignified and painful deaths.

Apart from being exclusive, the self-administration requirement is not strictly enforced and has been rendered essentially powerless. For instance, patients receive medication administration assistance, and their assistants have not been prosecuted for doing so. However, states continue to require self-administration (Thyden, 2017, p. 422). Many conditions may limit a patient's ability to move, such as Parkinson's Disease, bone cancer, brain cancer, genetic disorders, and motor vehicle accidents.

Patients should be able to delegate the physical act of administration to a person of their choosing. To ease physicians' concerns that assisted administration may lead to physician-administered euthanasia, the state of California should enact safeguards that prevent such scenarios, such as documentation-related requirements. For instance, the state of California could require meticulously reported documentation regarding who has been granted permission to assist with the drug administration. Additionally, assistants could be required to call or notify a doctor before the actual administration to ensure transparency in the medication administration process. Requiring a form with two witnesses' signatures could demonstrate that a patient ingested drugs voluntarily. Although this provision may appear insensitive given the emotionally charged nature of suicide, such a measure may be necessary to ensure proper legal standards are carefully followed (443-444).

Even if California legislators seem to be aware of this situation, there is still much room for improvement. While it is true that the self-administration requirement is not always enforced, it is still an official prerequisite. It can prevent a patient from successfully using the California End of Life Option Act, prolonging their suffering.

Nevertheless, it is worth mentioning that California Governor Newsom signed SB 380 in October 2021, which made significant changes to California's End of Life Option Act and went into effect on January 1, 2022. These changes included reducing the required waiting period between a patient's oral requests from 15 days to 48 hours. The self-administration requirement is still active. The new bill states that self-administration means a qualified individual's affirmative, conscious, and physical act of administering and ingesting the aid-in-dying drug to bring about their own death (Coalition for Compassionate Care of California, 2021).

## 8. Real-Life Cases

In the case of Barbara Houck, a terminally ill Oregonian resident suffering during the terminal stages of Amyotrophic lateral sclerosis (ALS) also known as Lou Gehrig's disease, her son mixed her prescribed life-ending drugs into a bowl of pudding and spoon-fed it to her as per her request. Even though she had the right to tell him not to give her the drugs, they had been prescribed, and she made the conscious choice to die on her own terms (Thyden, 2017, pp. 444–445). Legislation should make the process easier and more comfortable for all people who wish to die through legal means while still preventing abuses, such as murder and coercion. The California End of Life Option Act self-administration requirement that is currently written into the law serves no real purpose and lacks practical enforceability.

According to the California Department of Public Health, prescriptions have been written for 2,858 people in California under the act. Between June 9, 2016, when the law came into effect, and December 31, 2020, 1,816 individuals, or 63.5%, had died from ingesting the drugs. The median age of the user was 74 years.

After carefully analyzing the testimonies of those who used the law and those who could not use it, Kim Callinan (2020) stresses that access is the remaining challenge regarding the California End of Life Option Act. Eligible patients are unable to access the law because of unnecessary regulatory requirements. The cumbersome 13-step process to use the law is challenging to complete for many California residents. The law's most cited problematic provision was the 15-day waiting period, which the legislation required before doctors could write the prescription. One-third of terminally ill patients in California who requested the option of medical aid in dying were unable to complete the process due to this requirement, according to a study by Kaiser Permanente Southern California published by the *Journal of the American Medical Association* (*JAMA*). For instance, to address this issue, the Oregon legislature amended its law (SB579) to permit doctors to waive the 15-day waiting period if the patient's death is imminent.

Nevertheless, it is important to mention that the 15-day waiting period has been reduced to 48 hours as of January 1, 2022. As Patrick McGreevy (2021) reported, California lawmakers approved changes to legislation to speed up and simplify the state process for terminally ill patients who are close to death to obtain prescriptions for lethal doses of drugs. Assemblyman Jim Wood (D-Healdsburg) told his colleagues during a floor discussion of SB-380[9] that he knew people who had suffered challenging and painful deaths without utilizing

---

[9] The bill also eliminated the requirement for a second, written attestation by the patient, which some families considered offensive.

the end-of-life law. State Sen. Susan Talamantes Eggman (D-Stockton) said the process in the California 2016 bill takes too long and that some patients are dying in pain before they can even obtain a prescription. Around 1,000 terminally ill adults who requested the use of the law died before completing the time-consuming process to use the California End of Life Option Act, almost the same number of people who have used the law. This new provision should make using the law more convenient for eligible patients.

Another challenge with the California End of Life Option Act, according to data, is related to healthcare provider participation. Patients have reported difficulty finding providers willing to engage in the end-of-life process. According to a survey of California hospitals published in the *Journal of Palliative Medicine*, close to two-thirds of California hospitals (64%) and almost all religious hospitals (97%) forbid their physicians from writing assisted suicide prescriptions. Several states have addressed this challenge by recognizing that other types of healthcare providers are qualified to participate in the law.

While relatively few people ultimately decide they need medical aid in dying (less than 1% of the population), data confirm that significant numbers benefit from the resulting improvements in choice and end-of-life care that come with the implementation of the euthanasia-related law. These facts suggest that it is essential to keep outlining ways to improve the California End of Life

Option Act to improve the quality of life in the state. Not only should legislators revise the self-administration requirement, but they should also encourage higher levels of health provider participation. California legislators seem to be aware that it is time to remove unnecessary barriers to aid in dying so that all eligible terminally ill individuals can retain their right to autonomy and can die with dignity in the manner they wish.

# References

California Department of Public Health. (2021). *California End of Life Option Act 2020 data report.* https://www.cdph.ca.gov/Programs/ CHSI/CDPH%20Document%20Library/CDPH_End_of_ Life_Option_Act_Report_2020_FINAL.pdf?TSPD_101_R0=0 87ed344cfab2000d45f75f0a25b72cd5df0d5e63446bc8ede245 8e14391b317cd228528f1354cdb08d03618f2143000ce9edad5 3ef0e477f300d68558adfa4ddbf6297b2b950e000aef42b10751 34fbd99da5f452b98f7298e4485a26c152e1

Callinan, K. (2020, March 31). *Access is challenge with California End of Life Option Act, not abuse.* Compassion and Choices. https:// compassionandchoices.org/news/access-is-challenge-with- california-end-of-life-option-act-not-abuse-2/

Coalition for Compassionate Care of California. (2021). *California End of Life Option Act.* https://coalitionccc.org/CCCC/Resources/End- of-Life-Option-Act/CCCC/Resources/End-of-Life-Option-Act. aspx?hkey=7d8f6da9-f29c-4ce8-b467-cc9d4bd08c31

Emanuel, E. J. (1994). The history of euthanasia debates in the United States and Britain. *Annals of Internal Medicine, 121*(10), 793–802. https://doi.org/10.7326/0003-4819-121-10-199411150-00010

Emanuel, E. (2017). Euthanasia and physician-assisted suicide: Focus on the data. *The Medical Journal of Australia, 206*(8), 339–340. https://doi.org/10.5694/mja16.00132

Fernandes, A. K. (2001). Euthanasia, assisted suicide, and the philosophical anthropology of Karol Wojtyla. *Christian bioethics: Non-Ecumenical Studies in Medical Morality, 7*(3), 379–402. https://doi.org/10.1076/chbi.7.3.379.6878

Jennings, P. K., & Talley, C. R. (2003). A good death?: White privilege and public opinion: Research on euthanasia. *Race, Gender & Class, 10*(3), 42–63. http://www.jstor.org/stable/41675087

Jonsen, A. R. (1978). Dying right in California — The Natural Death Act. *Clinical Toxicology, 13*(4), 513–522. https://doi.org/10.3109/15563657808988256

McGreevy, P. (2021, September 10). California lawmakers vote to speed process for terminally ill to end lives. *Los Angeles Times*. https://www.latimes.com/california/story/2021-09-10/california-lawmakers-vote-to-speed-up-and-simplify-ability-of-terminally-ill-to-end-their-lives

Myers, R. S. (2002). Physician-Assisted suicide and euthanasia in the United States: A Current legal perspective. In J. W. Koterski (Ed.), *Life and Learning XI: The proceedings of the Eleventh University Faculty for Life Conference* (pp. 3–27). University Faculty for Life. https://ssrn.com/abstract=2093660

Oregon Health Authority. (2021). *Oregon Death with Dignity Act 2020 data summary*. https://www.oregon.gov/oha/PH/PROVIDERPARTNERRESOURCES/EVALUATIONRESEARCH/DEATHWITHDIGNITYACT/Documents/year23.pdf

Rae, S. B. (1992). The California Euthanasia Initiative. *The Linacre Quarterly, 59*(4), 5–14. https://doi.org/10.1080/00243639.1992.11878175

Reis de Castro, M. P., Antunes, G. C., Marcon, L. M. P., Andrade, L. S., Rückl, S., & Andrade, V. L. Â. (2016). Eutanásia e suicídio assistido em países ocidentais: Revisão sistemática [Translated title in English]. *Revista Bioética, 24*(2), 355–367, https://doi.org/10.1590/1983-80422016242136

Thyden, A. M. (2017). Death with dignity and assistance: A critique of the self-administration requirement in California's End of Life Option Act. *Chapman Law Review, 20*(2), 421–446. https://digitalcommons.chapman.edu/cgi/viewcontent.cgi?article=1404&context=chapman-law-review

World Health Organization. (n.d.). *Palliative care.* https://www.who.int/health-topics/palliative-care

[63] Sims D. P. (2007). Out of control: What can we learn from the end of Massachusetts rent control? Journal of Urban Economics 61 129–151.

[64] US Department of Housing and Urban Development, Office of Community Planning and Development, The 2019 Annual Homeless Assessment to Congress, pp. 12, 68.

# About the Author

**D**r. Rodgir Cohen is a University Lecturer residing in Redlands, California. As a combat veteran and community activist, his research focuses on political science, ethics, and religious studies. Dr. Cohen's recent books include topics in California Government, American Political Science, and World Religions. Dr. Cohen has a passion for social justice to create a better world through actions and words. When he is not lecturing, he often can be found at the beach, at a unique coffee bar, or traveling and visiting new places.

CPSIA information can be obtained
at www.ICGtesting.com
Printed in the USA
BVHW040607110422
633385BV00002B/8